Linda Campbell Franklin

LIBRARY DISPLAY IDEAS

McFarland & Company, Inc.,
Publishers
Jefferson, N.C., 1980

LIBRARIAN BROWSING

Library of Congress Cataloging in Publication Data

Franklin, Linda Campbell.
Library display ideas.

Includes index.
1. Library exhibits. I. Title.
Z717.F73   025.5'2'028   80-17036
ISBN 0-89950-008-0
ISBN 0-89950-009-9 (pbk.)

for

Daddy, Mummy, and Robbie

Preface

I have been both a librarian and a display artist, but what I really am underneath it all is a reader, and a person who wants to do everything possible to help you entice readers into your library. The only form of advertising you as a librarian have, outside of word-of-mouth, is display. Therefore, displays must be made as interesting as possible, within the limits of budget and resources, and they must be changed frequently—as often as once a week.

Librarians have the opportunity (in fact, I'd see it as a pleasurable duty) to broaden the education and interests of the population they serve. In schools this can mean offering large measures of books which help to counter-balance textbooks that seem to be slow to break out of sexual, racial and other stereotypical molds. Books—fiction and nonfiction—are available on every subject and can provide a glimpse of changing and developing ideas. The intent of this book on displays is not to give instruction in book ordering, of course, but to encourage you to apply imagination and time to the presentation of books and the encouragement of reading. You have unlimited opportunities to express through your displays such concepts as understanding of others, honesty, respect, common sense, humor and love. You're selling a great product: the written word!

I know that librarians have many ideas about what will sell reading, but I hope that the displays in this book will nevertheless be helpful—especially as catalysts for your own ideas. I would love to receive snapshots of your displays, including interpretations and adaptations of my designs. I had so much fun doing the book that I can't help but believe that you are going to enjoy making everything real. Write me in care of the publisher.

Linda Campbell Franklin
New York City

Contents

Introduction

How to Use This Book

Please look at the whole book, including the appendices. You will see that here and there are directions for certain techniques which are applicable to other displays. These techniques, such as papier-mâché, mobiles, etc., are indexed.

The display ideas are arranged in several parts. The first covers the basics—materials and techniques useful for all the displays suggested. The next, Part II, is chronological and is based on the school year. Part III covers ideas related to general reading encouragement; the next part is one meant to be browsed for ideas of all kinds. Then Part V relates specifically to health and well-being topics and finally, there is a Part VI to be used when other than display cases and bulletin boards are involved.

There are two appendices. Appendix A is an Events Calendar listing 12 months' worth of important, display-worthy events particularly suitable to the school or public library setting. Appendix B: Manufacturers and Distributors gives full information on the several good sources for materials of all kinds mentioned in text, with complete ordering information and other tips.

The subject index will give you the page number of any display. Look it up by theme, subject or holiday.

The Recipe. After finding a display you wish to make, read the list of materials, and assemble all of them before starting to work. You may wish to reserve a book truck for this purpose, although there are some large items which will not fit on a truck.

Most of the displays can be made in about an hour—particularly after you have had a little practice in planning and making. One time-saving tip: do a letter count before cutting out the words used in a headline. Often one or more letters appear several times in one display, and all can be cut at once. Another important tip is to remove all the elements of each display as carefully as possible. After a few weeks you will have a very useful stock of materials (particularly cut-out letters and background papers) sorted and stored in a cupboard or closet.

Gridding Up. If you are worried about translating the drawings in this book into full-scale displays, use one of two methods. The system requiring the least equipment but the most care is the grid system. Lightly pencil in blue or red a half-inch or one-inch grid over my pictures. Draw in soft black pencil, a two-, three- or even five- or six-inch grid on the paper you wish to make your enlargement on. (See the drawing.)

Projecting an Enlargement. The second method requires an overhead or opaque projector. Lay the page with your chosen display design on the "stage" of the projector (or, in some cases, put the projector on the picture) and project an enlarged image onto a piece of paper temporarily taped to the wall. There are some extremely inexpensive mini-projectors of the opaque type available.

Customize. I suggest that you make notes, right on the pages of this book, about how you want to improve or change the display in the future. The addition of just one thing which would mean a lot to your audience—for example, a school symbol or mascot, or a change in color—may make a great difference in response to the display.

The Whole Book and Nothing But? A common quandary is whether or not to use real books in a display. It is obvious that a book that is actually on display cannot be checked out by a reader.

Dust jackets are invaluable, colorful, next-to-weightless additions to a display. You are ahead if you have been saving, and keeping organized, the dust jackets from books which arrive with them. Sometimes you might put a dust jacket on a same-size discard book for dimension.

If a book does not have a dust jacket, or if it cannot be removed, make a photocopy of the title page (or cover), or reproduce it in hand-lettering on a piece of colored paper the size of the book. You may want to make a number of dummy books like the drawings shown on page xii. These book designs

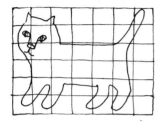

GRID BLOWUP

FIRST draw light grid lines over the picture you want to enlarge. MAKE SURE you measure exactly on grid. Then draw another light grid, of much larger proportions on blank paper. SKETCH the drawing now on the big piece of paper.

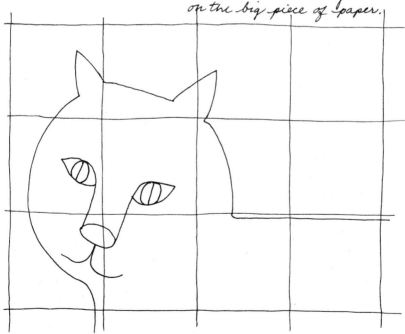

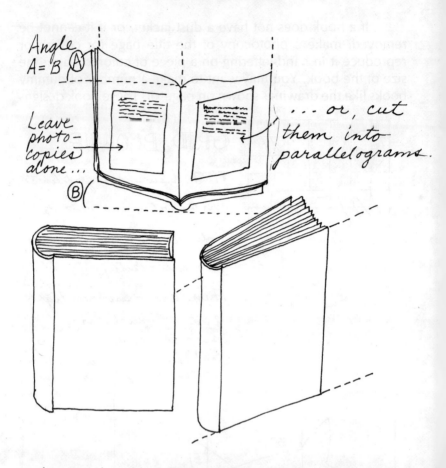

Angle
A = B

Leave
photo-
copies
alone...

... or, cut
them into
parallelograms.

can be reproduced by offset on different colors of paper, very inexpensively, or you can draw each one on colored construction paper. (See the drawings.)

Sometimes a useful substitute for a book can be made with a photocopy of a spread – two facing pages – which can be cut out and attached to colored paper.

Coordinate All the Displays? It is not a good idea to invest all your display space in one theme or idea. Exceptions might be for the beginning of the school year, when you are advertising your existence and hours to new students, or at holiday times. Before Christmas, for example, you may wish to make one display on the religious significance of the holiday, one on what is considered the commerical side (gift-giving, for example), and perhaps another which promotes recreational reading and study during the week or two of recess before school starts up in the new year. It is important to consider the feelings and beliefs of all your students and fellow workers, even if not everyone can be fully satisfied. Hanukkah, the Jewish Festival of Lights, often occurs quite close to Christmas, and should be included in your holiday-time display schedule.

People Colors. It is rarely possible to have more than one or two human figures in a display, so you will not often have a chance to represent a racial or ethnic mixture by using paper in several skin colors.

Two courses are open to you: you can rotate colors (such as beige, pink, tan and dark brown) and vary hair and eye colors; or you can use nothing but a fairly noncommittal, medium-tan paper – wrapping paper, say. Wrapping paper tan is sort of an abstract of all skin tones and various hair and eye colors can be used with it.

Who Does the Displays?

If you are typical of most school librarians, you will be doing most of the display work yourself, or with the help of your professional or clerical assistant(s). This may mean that one morning a week you have to go to school a bit early, or work after the library has closed.

Student Help. Because there is an enormous amount of work to do just keeping the library operating, you might look for student help. Find a student who can be given permission to work in the library on displays. This student need not be from the art teacher, but may come from a technical or trade school class, an English class, or from anywhere else. Try to arrange a way of giving credit for student help.

It is possible, however, that the art teacher may want to assign your display problems to one or more students, perhaps as often as once a month.

Faculty Cooperation

It is a good idea to exchange ideas, and talk about plans, with the teachers on the staff. Most of them will have teaching plans prepared and often a special assignment or project will be the perfect theme for a display.

In addition, you may need to borrow things from staff sometimes. Cultivate the interest of the shop teacher (who may help you saw, drill or paint, if needed), the art teacher, and the drama teacher. Librarians of public libraries can encourage local business people and professionals to coordinate displays in their windows with yours. The director of the local repertory theatre, chamber music society, or glass-collector's club may also want to share.

Types of Display Units

The displays in this book are meant for several types of displays units. The two most important of these are the bulletin board and the display window or case. The others are easel-back showcards for desk or table top, free-standing (or hanging) displays, standards, displays for the floor, exhibit cases, corkboard cases, pegboard racks or screens, letter boards, and even the edges of shelving and columns or posts.

As long as it doesn't interfere with overseeing the activity in the library, or use up too much space, there is practically no limit to the places where a display can be installed. You may even wish to photocopy a successful small bulletin board display and put copies around on study carrels.

The designs in this book are often adaptable to another mode—made three-dimensional for a window, or made of cut-out colored paper for a bulletin board.

Part I
THE BASICS

Materials

The following is a list of all the materials mentioned in the directions for displays. Some are rarely used. Others, marked with an asterisk, will be needed frequently. The largest single class of material is paper, especially background sheets (which may be quite large), poster board, corrugated cardboard, and colored construction paper.

There is no reason why you cannot re-use many materials. This is especially practical for paper backgrounds, monofilament line, cut-outs such as grass, trees, letters and numbers, and Mylar or colored acetates. Many of the designs in this book contain elements such as animals or human figures that are versatile.

There is also nothing to stop you from substituting materials you have on hand for those listed in the directions. This is particularly true of papers. Some alternative papers which can be used successfully (and are perhaps even better than the originals) are wallpaper, shelf paper, brown wrapping paper on a large roll (get the right width for your display windows or cases), florists' wrapping paper on a roll; the tail end of a large roll of newsprint paper from the local newspaper, gift wrap, outdated maps, newspapers, and crepe paper.

*Large sheets of colored paper, to fit bulletin board and window; one type is the sign paper which comes 107" wide in many colors.
*Poster boards in light blue, red, yellow, bright green, pale green, white, black, orange, and any other color you'd like.

*Colored construction paper, 9" x 12" or preferably 24" x 36".
*Felt tip pens and markers in black, red, blue, brown, green — with wide nibs (finer nibs useful too).
*Grease pencils in black, red, white, yellow, etc.
*Set of crayons with many colors.
*Masking tapes, ½" and 1" white — used because it can usually be removed without damaging whatever it is stuck to; also
*Double-face masking tape, ½" width is fine.
*Soft lead sketching pencil.
*Kneaded and art gum erasers.
*Staple gun.
*White household glue.
*Razor blades, single-edge.
*Paper cutter — at least 12" x 12".
*X-Acto knives — No. 1 for light-medium work; No. 2 for medium to heavy work. Keep several extra blades on hand.
*Mat knife — heavy duty for cutting cardboard and corrugated cardboard.
*Pin-back 3-D plastic letters are invaluable because of the time they save in lettering. They are somewhat expensive, but I believe they are well worth their cost. Two sizes would be most useful — a ¾" and 1½" for bulletin boards; a 1¾" and a 2½" for display windows. Futura upper case is probably the best style.
*Diecut display letters of heavy cardboard are also good. These are not as expensive as the pin-backs, but the fonts — the sets of letters distributed according to average use — are just as good. Diecuts may be attached with double-face tape and most can be wiped off if soiled.
*Diecut letters of thin paper. These are very useful, and at least one company (see Appendix B) makes sets in patterned paper. **Note:** Of course, all pre-cut or formed letters can be replaced by letters which you cut yourself from any kind of paper.
*Paper scissors.
*Rulers — a yardstick, a tape measure and a metal-edge rule.

*Push Pins.
*Monofilament fishing line, one reel.
*Spools of heavy-duty black and white thread.
*Styrofoam forms—several sizes of balls (from 4" to 8"), and perhaps other interesting geometric forms. The dimestore stocks these around Christmas time; they are also usually available from florists' supply companies, or may be ordered from a plastic supply house.
*Velcro fasteners—dressmakers' strips and a few packages of the dots. Black, white, tan are the most useful colors.
*Paint—poster and/or acrylic in tube or jar.
*Brushes—½" and 1¼" flat showcard style for lettering, plus various round and "bright" sizes.
*Pipecleaners—assorted colors and white.
*Straight pins.
Map pins, black, or
Glass-headed pins.
Dressmaker's T-shaped long pins.
Clay kitty litter, four-pound bag.
Balloons, one bag assorted.
Small rocks.
Colored felt pieces, 9" x 12", from the dime store. White, black, red, green, bright yellow, blue, purple are all useful colors. Many of the bulletin board ideas could be made almost entirely from colored felt pieces.
Pinking shears.
Dacron fiberfill—a couple of yards or so, or
Cotton batting.
Fabric remnants in varied colors or patterns for backgrounds. A large piece of black velvet or velveteen is especially useful.
Coathangers.
Heavy wire.
Wire cutters.
Pliers.
Hole punch.
Nails—assortment.

Newspapers and old magazines.
Wallpaper paste.
Wig form—Styrofoam head.
Colored acetate or Mylar film, wide rolls or sheets.
Yarn—fairly heavy, several colors.
Used, gray string mop.
Burned out lightbulbs.
Jointed skeleton figure of cardboard, 30″ or 55″ high.
Scrap boards, preferably 1″ x 8″ or 1″ x 12″.
Dowel rods, ¼″, several at least 36″ long.
Assorted cartons and boxes (needed for their cardboard as well
   as in their original form. If you look through the book for
   those displays requiring corrugated cardboard or boxes,
   then you can keep an eye out for the right sizes).
Aluminum foil.
Waxed paper.
Foil stars.
Black, brown, blue, white simple plastics buttons for eyes.

Sources

    As a display artist you will have to—and want to—depend
on a combination of store-bought art and craft supplies, on
found objects and materials, and on borrowed objects.
    Store-bought. Display materials are most easily found in
stationery stores, school supply dealers, artists' supply stores,
and through library and office suppliers. See Appendix B at the
back of the book.
    Discards. You will always have your eye open for
something which can be made use of in your displays. Don't be
afraid to ask for what you want. Often yours will be the only
request for something that would otherwise be discarded—a
three-dimensional, honeycombed tissue paper pineapple at
the grocer's; a vacuum-formed plastic snowman at the liquor
store; a perfectly good scrap of ¼″ plywood at the hardware or
lumber dealer; and used (but nearly good as new) colored
seamless paper, which comes in extremely wide rolls, from the
local photography studio. Build a network of these suppliers,

and you may soon find that the grocer himself is even coming up with display ideas for you!

Then think about what you or your family throw out each day. What about that white or gold plastic egg which is the container for a famous brand of pantyhose? Wouldn't a big basket of those be the start of an interesting display? What about the colorful pages of magazines, which could be cut into letters, or made into collage backgrounds? Try, for example, cutting out all the pictures of mouths you find in ads or illustrations before throwing a magazine away, then paste them all, crazy quilt fashions, to a piece of poster board. You immediately have the background for a display of books on languages, health care, love or communication.

Scavenging. Being a New Yorker, it is almost second nature for me to scavenge the streets and sidewalks. It may take you some time to comfortably help yourself to useful odds and ends you see thrown out, but keep in mind your fine purpose! You will find it easier, probably, if you are not alone, so recruit a helper or a scout.

Good materials are to be found in the street, sidewalk or at the back entrances of stores at shopping centers or downtown malls. Styrofoam packing materials — either the formed hunks which fit around such things as televisions or dehumidifiers, or the peanut-shaped loose pellets used in mailing small fragile things are all useful. Blister packing, that clear vinyl sheet with bubbles, also has potential. So do the hoses from worn out vacuum cleaners (think robots or monsters), long tubes from carpet rolls or wrapping paper, huge glass jars which once held restaurant mayonnaise or pickles (fill with seashells, rocks, small dolls, toy cars, etc., for unexpected effects) — the possibilities are endless.

Art and Craft Techniques

There are many tricks to help you prepare displays, from handling a brush to cutting out chains of paper dolls. Techniques not explained under the directions for a particular display (such as papier-mâché) are found below.

Brushwork and Painting. Occasionally you will want to paint a large surface—a cardboard carton, or background paper. Suit the brush to the job: use a wide flat brush for large areas, and buy a fairly good one that won't leave too many hairs in the paint. Use water-based paint, and clean your brush with soapy water immediately after use. If you feel timid about using a brush to make complicated lines or detailed patterns, either sketch out the basics of what you want with pencil before painting, or use a felt tip pen to draw the outlines to be filled in with paint.

Splatter effects are obtained by shaking a brush loaded with paint; don't load it too full, or there will be many large puddles and only a few splatters.

A short-bristled oil-painting brush, which is stiff, will serve you the same way a broad nib felt pen does.

Felt Tip Pens and Markers. These are good to have in both the fine point and slanted broad nib. Fine points are used for detail work in small scale displays such as bulletin boards. The broad nib markers, which come in such a wonderful array of colors, can be used for making outlines or coloring displays.

Paper Cutouts. Many of my display designs use simple

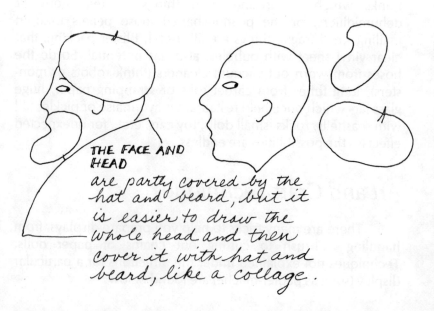

THE FACE AND HEAD are partly covered by the hat and beard, but it is easier to draw the whole head and then cover it with hat and beard, like a collage.

paper cutouts, because they are a way of gaining some of the effects of three dimensions, and they are easy to do.

Cut-out Lettering. The more exact and ornate the lettering, the harder it is to get it to look good. My technique for lettering works both for cutouts and painted or inked letters. I couldn't do it without a soft drawing pencil, which can be easily erased.

Make your lines as light as you can, and make a bottom line, a top line and some vertical lines with a ruler. Then, quickly draw the shapes of the letters. Speed, believe it or not, will give fluency to the lines. Refine any mistakes in width or edges, then cut out. Cut-out letters have two important advantages. They can be recycled, and they are easy to space.

Cut-out Figures and Objects. At least at first, it is easiest to cut out seen and unseen parts of faces, arms, legs, etc. Any mistakes you make in judging just how the puzzle fits together are avoided. Instead of putting a jigsaw puzzle together, you are making a collage. A good example of what I mean is shown in the face opposite.

Adding Dimension. When using paper cutouts, or other lightweight additions to a bulletin board or display

background, you can add a bit of dimension two ways. First, you can fit little squares of corrugated cardboard behind the cutouts (glue or doubleface tape the squares to your cutout first, then to the background); or you can form a little bulge or bowing-out when you glue or tape down the corners or

SPACING and sketching of letters
is easy if you do it fairly quickly
with a soft pencil. Whatever happens,
don't worry. Minor mistakes are very
unimportant.

ABC
DEM
RWY

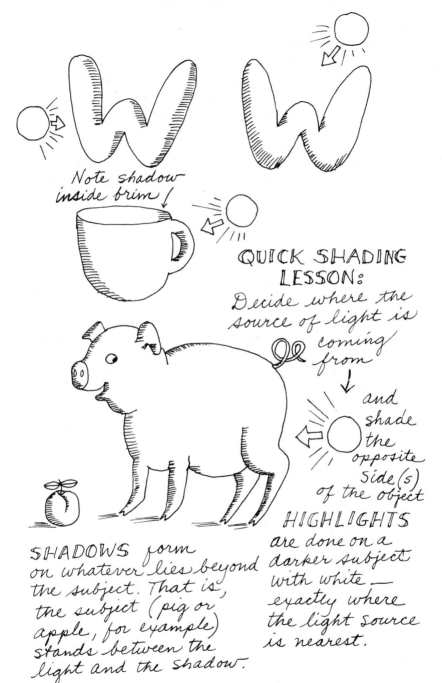

Note shadow inside brim

QUICK SHADING LESSON:
Decide where the source of light is coming from

↓

and shade the opposite side(s) of the object

HIGHLIGHTS are done on a darker subject with white — exactly where the light source is nearest.

SHADOWS form on whatever lies beyond the subject. That is, the subject (pig or apple, for example) stands between the light and the shadow.

edges of your cutout. See the drawings. The *illusion* of dimension can be created by drawing shading lines.

Folded Paper Multiples. There are two basic kinds of multiple cutouts, the chain, and the centered design. The chain can be done with from three to 16 or more figures or forms, depending on the paper used. Very coarse, thick or fairly inflexible paper is good for up to five or six figures; thin paper, or crepe paper, is needed for more.

Chain Gang. Very carefully fold your paper in accordian pleats. Make sure all the left folds and all the right folds line up with each other. Draw your design, making sure that there are two uncut spots (your hinges) on both left edge and right edge. It is sometimes easiest to make cutting accurate if you trim top and bottom close to your design, and secure all the folds with a heavy paperclip. Now carefully scissor out your design. Final touches can be made with a paper punch, although this usually works best for fewer than eight layers of paper.

Center Fours. All kinds of four-sided, or four-part designs and forms can be cut this way. Fold the paper in half and then in quarters. You can work with either square or rectangular paper. Draw your design, making sure that the centers are cut out, and that the folded edges have at least two "hinge" points, or that the center is intact. (See page 34.)

Making Eyes. Eyes are used by cartoonists to express all kinds of emotions. Everything depends on the shape, the slant,

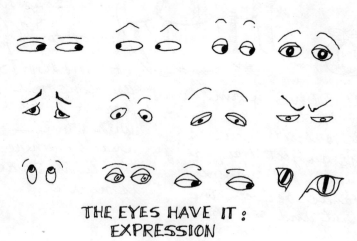

THE EYES HAVE IT :
EXPRESSION

PAPER DOLL
CHAINS

Leave Ⓐ, Ⓑ, Ⓒ and
Ⓓ attached at edge to
form the chain.

Cut away cross-hatched
areas.

the positioning, the pupils, and the placement of the eyebrows. When you are drawing eyes, try putting your own face in the same expression you are trying to draw, and you will really find it easier to draw it right.

The Velcro Pinch. This is the technique used for securing monofilament line to the sides or back of the display case, or the ceiling of the library. Velcro fasteners are available in small pairs of dots, nickel-sized dots, and various ribbon lengths. Velcro may be bought in the notions departments of stores.

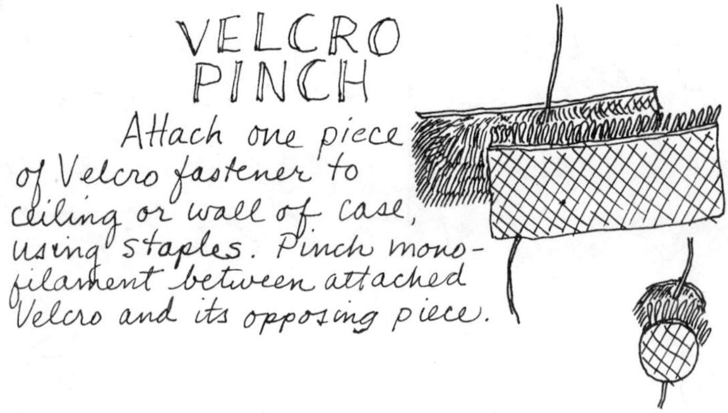

VELCRO
PINCH
Attach one piece
of Velcro fastener to
ceiling or wall of case,
using staples. Pinch monofilament between attached
Velcro and its opposing piece.

Part II

MONTH-BY-MONTH

Student Volunteer

Recruiting student help for displays.
Bulletin board.

Materials: blue background paper
white paper
cut-out or pin-back "WANTED"
brown felt pen

Technique: Glue one white cloud in place, lower right. Draw ladder and student and small letters. Part of the ladder will be drawn over the cloud. Attach other cloud and headline letters.

School's Open!

First week of school; general reading.
Display case.

Materials: background paper
green, red, white construction paper
carton, approximately 7½" x 9" x 6" high
book, approximately 7" x 9" long, or the same
   length as the carton
masking tape
monofilament line
brick red poster paint
black felt marker
wide paint brush
fall leaves
white glue
several small colorful books
strip of corrugated cardboard, about 9" long

Technique: Paint the carton and let dry. Cut front doors, as shown in the picture. Draw window panes on white paper and glue to sides. Use the strip of corrugated cardboard to make a triangle, which is used to hold the book open at about a 40 or 45 degree angle. Use masking tape, not the extremely sticky kind but the white used by artists, to tape the triangle inside the book. Make a green "shingled" roof for the book, then hang suspended over the open carton. Arrange letters on background paper; put small books in the carton; arrange leaves and card with hours.

Adaptation: Hang the roof a bit higher, put message on the roof, and use on file or desk top to dispense book marks, etc.

Welcome to Our House

Library hours; start of school year; general reading.
Small display case.

Materials: background paper
two 3″ or 4″ Styrofoam balls
9″ x 12″ felt rectangles, contrasting colors
pipecleaners
yellow, brown or black yarn
stiff paper
felt marker
glass-head pins, blue or black
3″ pencil, stick or ½″ dowel rod
small black button
several broomstraws
cut-out letters

Technique: Cut out stiff paper arms and a tail, as shown in the drawing. Use the contrasting colors (say brown and white) of felt to make the dog's body. You can cut out the space between the dog's legs if you wish, or draw the outline of the legs with the felt marker. The dog's head is complete with broomstraw whiskers, black button nose, pin eyes and pipecleaner ears. Attach to the spine of the book with a pencil or coffee stirrer, etc., and masking tape. Cover the end of the tail in felt, and insert tightly, like a bookmark, in the book. The hair of the human book figure is made of yarn. Insert by pushing tip of short yarn lengths into the Styrofoam ball with the point of a pencil.

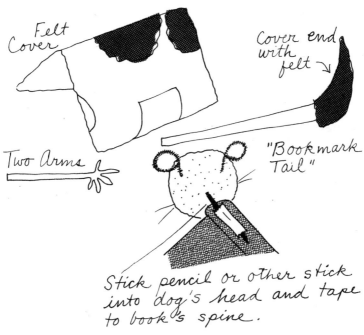

Stick pencil or other stick into dog's head and tape to book's spine.

Welcome to the Library!

Introduction to the library services; general reading.

Small display case.

Materials: blue background paper
green floor paper
large book
crayons or felt pens
construction paper, various colors
cardboard

Technique: Put up background paper and attach clouds. Cut out the bookmark figures and color the features and clothing details. Insert into the propped book, using tape to secure if necessary. Make the easel-back tree of cardboard.

Adaptation: Make this a bulletin board display by using a cut-out book shape instead of a real book, and a cut-out tree minus the easel back.

Library Cards

Football season; circulation drive; sports books.

Display case.

Materials: blue background, green ground paper
paper in school color
football
toothpicks
scissor-curled colored paper
crayons or felt pens
several football passes
several library cards
cut-out or pin-back letters

Technique: Cut out chain of spectators from school color and draw details in with constrasting color. Attach to background. Make toothpick pennants. Arrange sports book, football, paper curls, cards and tickets. Put up headline and clouds.

Adaptation: This is a simple bulletin board display, by substituting a cut-out football for the real one. Everything else can remain the same.

YOUR LIBRARY CARD IS A TICKET TOO

Draw on the clothes, etc.

ALTERNATIVES:

YOUR LIBRARY CARD IS A PASS TO MORE THAN ONE SEASON

YOU CAN GET A YEAR'S TICKET TO THE LIBRARY

SUPPORT OUR TEAM AND OUR LIBRARY TOO

Football

Football season; biographies of football stars.

Bulletin board.

Materials: green background paper
brown, tan, white, and school colors construction paper
black felt pen

Technique: Cut out four legs, two each in your school colors
and two in the colors of the biggest rival. The
hand is tan. The shoes are brown and so is the
football. Draw details like the dots for the pigskin,
the lacing, the stitching on the legs with a felt pen.
Assemble the pieces on the background, then
draw the spikes along the bottom edge of the
shoes. Use this board near the sports books, or
assemble a number of sports books on a table and
use this design for an easel-back sign.

CHECK OUT SOME KNUTE BOOKS!

Four pant legs, two each in your school colors & those of other team. Draw on padding stitches.

Four calves and socks. Reverse one pair and color stripes in other team's colors.

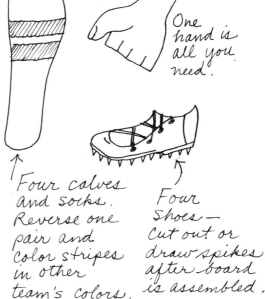

One hand is all you need.

Four shoes — Cut out or draw spikes after board is assembled.

Discovery of America

Combined Columbus Day and Leif Ericsson Day.

Bulletin board.

Materials: background paper
red, black, medium brown, yellow, tan, white
   construction paper
black felt tip pen
cut-out or pin-back letters

Technique: Faces and hands are cut from tan paper. You can
avoid the hands, if you find them difficult, by
having the two explorers put their hands behind
their backs. Columbus wears a red jacket and cap
and black pants. Ericsson has a brown furry-
looking shirt (use a felt pen to scribble the fur),
brown pants and a white and brown helmet.
Columbus has black hair; Ericsson has yellow.
When drawing the features, fill in the irises of
Columbus' eyes so that they are black. By not
filling in the iris circles of Ericsson's eyes, they will
seem lighter. Add the letters and the book jackets.

Warlock

Unusual words plus theme of sexual equality. Halloween.

Bulletin board.

Materials: orange background paper
black, dark green, pale green construction paper
strings from used gray mop
cut-out or pin-back letters

Technique: Cut out warlock's head and hands from pale green paper; cut his black clothes and the bat. Assemble on background. Add the letters and the equal rights flag. You can add some dimension to the fingers by curling them against the blade of a pair of sharp scissors.

Note: the dotted lines show joins of more than one sheet of paper if you plan to make this a large display.

Cookbook Witch

Halloween cookery.

Bulletin board.

Materials: background paper
black, tan, white, yellow, orange, pale green construction paper
cotton balls
several strands from used gray string mop
black felt tip pen
cut-out or pin-back letters
photocopies of two pages from a cookbook

Technique: Cut out witch's garb from black paper. Cut green
hands and face; yellow and orange flames; black
pot and bat; tan spoon. Assemble and add pulled-
out cotton balls for smoke puffs. Attach photocopy of cookbook pages to book shape, and put
up headline.

Macbeth's Witch

Tie-in with reading or performance of Macbeth.

Display case.

Materials: dark blue background paper
black, pale green and gray construction paper
dress form on a stand
lightweight wig form – head
fairly tall carton
double boiler
black choir or graduation robe
used, gray string mop
black and white poster paint
wide flat brush and small brush

Techniques: Put up background paper. Cut out moon and cloud from pale green and gray paper and attach. Paint three sides of carton with black paint, then draw stove leg and burner outlines in white. Position dress form and attach wig form head, with tape if necessary. Cut out nose and chin profile from pale green paper and draw details; attach to wig form. Add strands from mop. Dress witch in robe and cut-out hat. Green hand, taped inside sleeve, gets attached to handle of weighted double boiler. Arrange books and put speech balloon in place.

Ⓐ Glue the face cutout
to Styrofoam head and pin mop string
hair on; Ⓑ Cut out black half circle to
form cone of hat; and Ⓒ Cut irregular
black brim. Ⓓ One scraggly hand will do.

Basketball

Basketball season.
Display case.

Materials: black background paper
tan wrapping paper
orange or yellow paper for floor (or wood-grained
  shelf paper)
brown felt pen
Sytrofoam or hard rubber ball
monofilament line
blue poster paint or blue adhesive tape
glue
pipecleaner for Styrofoam ball, or
screw and screwdriver for rubber ball

Technique: Put up background and floor paper. Paint or tape
blue lines and semi-circle on floor. Cut 4 players
out as shown. Unfold and punch out eyes, and
draw or color in indications of features and
clothing. Fold tabs on feet, dab on glue, position
players and suspend ball above their circle. Make
pipecleaner screweye for Styrofoam, or actually
screw a real wood screw into hard rubber ball.

Use a piece
of paper
folded in
quarters. Cut
away the parts
shown dark at
left, and
leave the
hands
connected.

Happy Hanukkah

Introduce a Jewish holiday.
Window display; display case.

Materials: blue background paper
9-branch candelabra, the *menorah*
2 or 3 yards of white cloth, or a fine white tablecloth
medium-size cardboard carton
cut-out or pin-back letters
9 white candles
white poster paint
small rectangular sponge
3 x 5 card

Technique: Draw with a light pencil, two or three large, off-center circles. Using sponge dipped in paint and partly wrung out, brush paint out from edges of circles, as shown in drawing, to create a radiant effect. Dry thoroughly, although this shouldn't take long because if the paint is put on thickly or wetly, the paper will warp. Mount background. Set up carton and drape the white cloth. Set up the menorah with the candles. The menorah, by the way, sometimes has 8 branches, but never less. Attach the letters, add the card with the short text on this holiday, and arrange the books.

Comments: There are various spellings used for Hanukkah. These include *Chanukah* and *Hanukah*. You might adapt your spelling to whatever is favored by the reference books you have, or the books on customs which you feature in the display. **Suggestions for text:** Hanukkah is a Jewish religious holiday. It takes its name, "Festival (or Feast) of Lights," from the fact that it commemorates the victory of light over darkness, of spiritual independence over despotism, the victory of a

small handful of Jews against a Syrian king who tried to destroy their religion about 2000 years ago. The celebration lasts eight days, and each day another candle is lit, symbolizing the slow but steady victory of enlightenment.

Santa Claus' Winners

Christmas-time reading.
Column or wall display.

Materials: crepe paper bricks or corrugated paper bricks
cotton batting or dacron fiber batting
2 sheets pink or tan paper
large red poster board
black felt pen, broad nib
old mailbag or dark blue or gray laundry bag
gray cardboard

Technique: Wrap column with paper bricks, and if there is no border, make the chimney top from the gray cardboard. Cut Santa from red poster board; his face and hand are pink or tan. Pull batting apart into cuffs and beard, cap brim and eyebrows. Attach, and draw features. Put up letters and arrange bag with books beneath.

Adaptation: Cut shapes from colored paper, and make into a bulletin board with dust jackets.

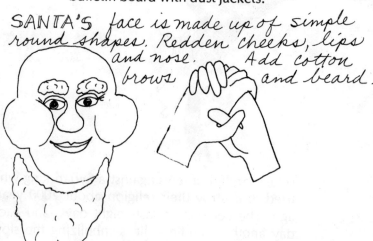

SANTA'S face is made up of simple round shapes. Redden cheeks, lips and nose. Add cotton brows and beard.

Christ Was a Gift

Christmas as a religious holiday.

Display case.

Materials: blue background paper
hay or straw
basket (even a dog or cat wicker bed)
baby doll, lifesize
white or cream cloth torn in long strips
cut-out or pin-back letters
double-face tape (or paste)
large silver foil star (can be made from aluminum foil)
larger white or pale blue paper star
books on Christian meaning of Christmas

Technique: Put up background paper. Attach large paper star, then put foil star centered on that. Arrange straw in basket, showing little of basket. Actually swaddle the doll in strips of cloth and lay in the straw bed. Put up the letters and arrange the books. Add a greeting from the library if you wish.

Adaptation: For a bulletin board, everything can be cut out of paper. The drawing shows how to make a realistic-looking basket. Blue, white, and tan are good colors for this display.

DRAWING A BASKET

1. Pencil lines in and mark "bricks"

2. Draw criss-crosses. Erase confusing lines

3. Fill in with more bands . . .

Cheat some and don't worry about "weaving" them

4. Ink lines; erase rest of pencil lines and draw texture lines.

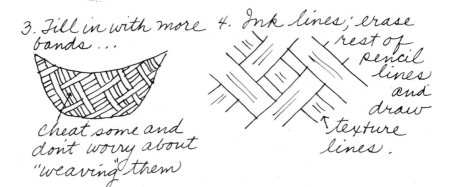

Gift Packages

Christmas-time book-reading or book-giving.
Bulletin board.

Materials: background paper
               2 or 3 colorful dust jackets
               gift ribbon
               cut-out or pin-back letters

Technique: Use book jackets as gift wrap, attach and arrange
               letters.

Christmas Vacation Reading

Encourage borrowing books over Christmas vacation.
Bulletin board.

Materials: background paper – perhaps tan or light blue
               broad nib felt pin
               cut-out or pin-back letters
               cut-out book or real dust jacket
               crayons or poster paint

Technique: This display can be done by drawing everything and coloring, or by cutting out the elements from colored paper, including gift wraps. You could make the background tan; tree green with red balls; girl's outfit in red, pillow in green. Her face and hands can also be tan; her hair brown, yellow or black.

Gift Books

Christmas-time book-giving.

Bulletin board.

Materials: background paper
green, red, brown, white construction paper
gold or silver star
several paper cut-out books
cut-out or pin-back letters
gift ribbon
black felt tip pen

Technique: Cut out green tree, as shown in the drawing. Cut out tree holder and book ornaments. Tape or glue to background paper and draw details on holder and movement and jetstream lines. You can add other details, such as an orange flame under the puffs of smoke, or stars and planets in the sky.

Comments: The books you do up as gifts can either be library books—on any subject, including making gifts and Christmas decorations—or suggestions for books to buy as gifts. You might cooperate with a local bookstore, and even include a list of good gift books. Remember that you are trying to encourage *reading*, not just circulation figures.

GIFT BOOKS REALLY GO FAST!

GIFTS YOU MAKE

GET ONE NOW

Cut slit

Draw screws

Book ornament for tree.

Piece of green paper folded in half.

Cut out an orange flame to put under the smoke puffs, if you wish.

Happy New Years

New Year's; customs; world religions/history.

Bulletin board.

Materials: background paper
felt tip pens
confetti or colored paper cut into strips and
small pieces
cut-out or pin-back letters

Techniques: This is a very simple display. It can be gussied up
by adding symbols of the various New Years, and
by adding the years of the different calendars.

You can also add a calendar with the Gregorian
dates equivalent to the others circled. The
Chinese calendar offers several colorful options—
a dragon's head, firecrackers, or the symbol for
the year—monkey, snake, rabbit, etc.
Gregorian 1981
Hebrew 5742
Chinese 4579
Islamic 1402

For Real

Valentine's Day; introducing books on loving.

Bulletin board.

Materials: background paper
tan, blue and red construction paper
double-face tape, or glue
black felt pen
cut-out or pin-back letters
book jackets

Technique: Put up background paper and arrange on it the cut-out shapes forming the two figures. Choose appropriate hairstyles. Draw hearts on the cut-out letters, cut out hearts and draw faces on them. Assemble with book jackets. *Note*: a white background, or red background is especially good for use on Valentine's Day.

Love Words

Encourage general reading and writing; books on word play, word origins; Valentine's Day.

Bulletin board.

Materials: blue background paper
tan, white, red, black or brown paper
magazine photography of a door
cut-out or pin-back letters
felt pen

Technique: Put up background paper. Cut out the simple faces of the two figures and draw the features on. (Or use suitable pictures from a magazine.) Cut out Cupid from tan (or pink) paper and color his red ribbon. Add the clouds and the speech balloon, the cut-out hearts and the letters.

Love and Affection

Books, fiction or nonfiction, on love, dating, marriage.

Bulletin board.

Materials:　background paper or fabric (maybe denim)
various colors of construction paper, or paper
　　with printed designs
colored paper for hair
pink, brown, tan paper for hands
double-face tape (or paste)
book jackets
red heart

Technique:　Put up background. Cut out couple's clothing. By
the way, the couple can be two girls or two boys;
leave out the heart and the subject is friendship.
Attach boy's pants; the girl's and the boy's tops are
interwoven. Tuck in hands. Add hair and book
jackets. No words are necessary.

Comments:　This is a good display for Judy Blume's books, or
for books such as Reingold's *How to Cope*.

Adaptation:　Use real clothing, at least for the shirts or
sweaters, and pin or staple carefully.

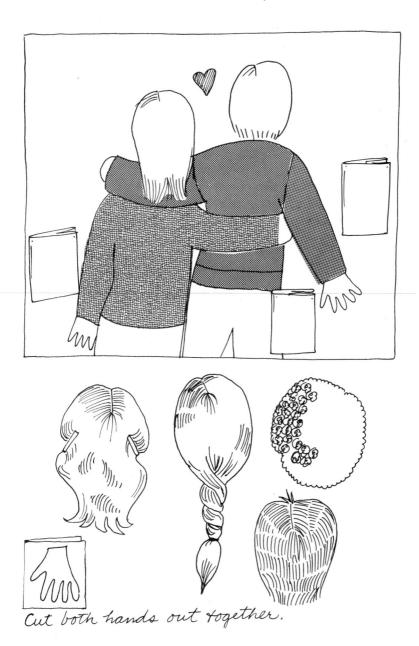

Cut both hands out together.

You Don't Have to Be Irish

St. Patrick's Day; general reading.

Bulletin board.

Materials: background paper
green, brown construction paper
pin-back or cut-out letters
black felt pen
book jackets

Technique: Draw large tree, without leaves, on brown paper. Draw lines for bark. Cut out items of clothing from green paper, drawing on details of buttons, stitching. Add as many things—muffler, gloves, sweater—as you wish. Use cut-out shamrocks, or shamrock stickers from stationery store.

Adaptation: For a case display, you can put real items of green clothing on a small, multi-branched tree limb. Use a Christmas tree stand to hold it, or prop it in corner.

Don't Fool Around: Read

April Fool's Day; encourage reading of any kind.
Bulletin board.

Materials: background paper   comic book
tan, green, yellow   magazine
     red constr. paper   cut-out or
newspaper   pin-back letters
cereal box   cut-out book
can label

Technique: From tan paper, cut out fool's head, upper torso and hands, all in one piece. Give him a yellow and red cap, green and red shirt, red or green pants and boots. Trace upper torso on red or green paper, then attach small squares or diamonds of the contrasting color to make the checkers. Then draw line for arm. Put up the various items to be read, and the headline.

Adaptation: Use tan background paper and draw the fool on with a felt pen. Use crayons or felt pens to color his clothes and book. Pin up various reading materials.

DRAWING TIP: this series of parallel lines make it easy to cut out jester's book.

NOTE: both of jester's legs and feet are the same shape, but put at a different angle.

Here's to the
Merrie Month of May!

May 1; gardening or flower arrangement; customs around the
world.

Ceiling or light fixture; column; display case.

Materials: (1) crepe paper streamers in pastel colors
monofilament line
basket with handle
artificial flowers
book jackets

            (2) for a variation, a 1″ dowel rod about 2′ long
a 5″ or 6″ square piece of ¼″ plywood
several small freestanding dolls & toys (or
provide stands)

Technique: (1) Twist crepe paper streamers, hang from a
central point (the light fixture, for example), and
tape other end to various points on the shelves.
Leave a good swag without interfering with
traffic in the library. Using monofilament or
cellophane tape hang book jackets and flowers.
Arrange, if desired, over a table with a basket
centerpiece and an
array of books and
flowers. (2) Screw
together a Maypole
(as shown). Wrap
dowel with crepe
paper. Make
streamers half the
width; attach them
with a thumbtack to
the rod. Give ends
to the hands or
paws of dolls or toy
animals, or swag
and twist and fasten
to sides of case.

SCREW the dowel to a piece of ¼″ plywood Cover base, if you want, with green felt.

MMMMMMMmm Good!

Biographies of mothers of famous people; being or becoming a mother; fiction; Mother's Day.

Bulletin board.

Materials: pale blue background paper
white paper
bright pink paper
wide felt pen, dark blue
several old fashion magazines
book jackets
cut-out or pin-back letters

Technique: Cut lips out of a good number of pictures in the magazines. Cut large pink lips, in exaggerated shape, leaving center open. Position big lips over white paper (don't draw in teeth, they tend to look awful in this size), paste down, and scatter-paste the smaller magazine lips—like butterflies—around the board. Attach cut-out letters for headlines; write the other words with the felt pen, and attach book jackets.

School's Out: Don't Take a Vacation from Reading

School's out; summer vacation; books on summer sports, etc. Display case.

Materials: light blue background paper
tan paper
large piece of corrugated cardboard
big sheets of white paper
heavy upholstery needle & thread
colorful towel
suntan lotion
pair of sunglasses
small vanity case or duffle bag
several paperback books
cut-out or pin-back letters
blue, red & brown felt pens, wide

Technique: Cut big book, with "wing" tip tops, as shown below. Sew (or use a thin line of glue) the pages to the cover, and fold along "spine." Punch two holes for earpieces of glasses. Tape cut-out tan hands to sides. Draw mouth in big red smile. Indicate waves on blue background. Position big book on towel, arrange case, paperbacks. Put up headline and crudely letter "See you in September" (or any other message) in the foreground on the sand. If you have a program for checking books out for the whole summer, type up an explanation and invitation and include in case.

EXAGGERATED
shape for book
cover and pages.

Curl fingers
around the
handle.

Freedom Through Books

Encourage general reading or introduce self-help books; Fourth
    of July.
Bulletin board.

Materials: blue background paper
red, white, tan paper
silver foil stars or aluminum foil
red, blue, black felt pens, broad nib
cut-out or pin-back letters
book jackets

Technique: Cut out Uncle Sam head and shoulders from tan
and white paper. Use felt pens to draw the stripes
and features. Attach to background. Cut wavy
stripes of red and white paper. You can cut all
five of them at the same time if you extend the
length of them. Attach to the background at an
angle, then trim off excess at the edges. Put up
stars and lettering, and arrange book jackets.
Note: Around the time of the Fourth of July
holiday, many stationery and card stores sell
paper decorations in the form of Uncle Sam, firecrackers, the flag, various buntings etc. These
can be added to this display very effectively.

Adaptation: This can be made into a case display by using a
full-length Uncle Sam figure—perhaps one of the
tall jointed versions. Put the figure in a running,
leaping or other free, joyful position, and use lots
of flags and stripes.

Part III

READING ENCOURAGEMENT

All Paths Lead To Us

General reading; introduction to the library services.

Small display case

Materials: green background and floor paper
red and tan construction paper
box the size of a big book
wind-up dolls or toys
cut-out or pin-back letters

Technique: Cover the box with paper binding. If the box you have is a perfectly good color for a book, choose another contrasting color for the partial binding and trim. Cut out a doorway and position pathway. Arrange dolls and put up headline.

All Roads Lead to the Library

Career books; general reading; library use.

Bulletin board.

Materials: green background paper
gray and white construction paper
felt pens
book jacket

Technique: Cut the roadways out of gray paper. If the bulletin
board is large, you may have to piece sheets of
paper together as shown below. Attach the road
signs and make a roof for the bookjacket library.

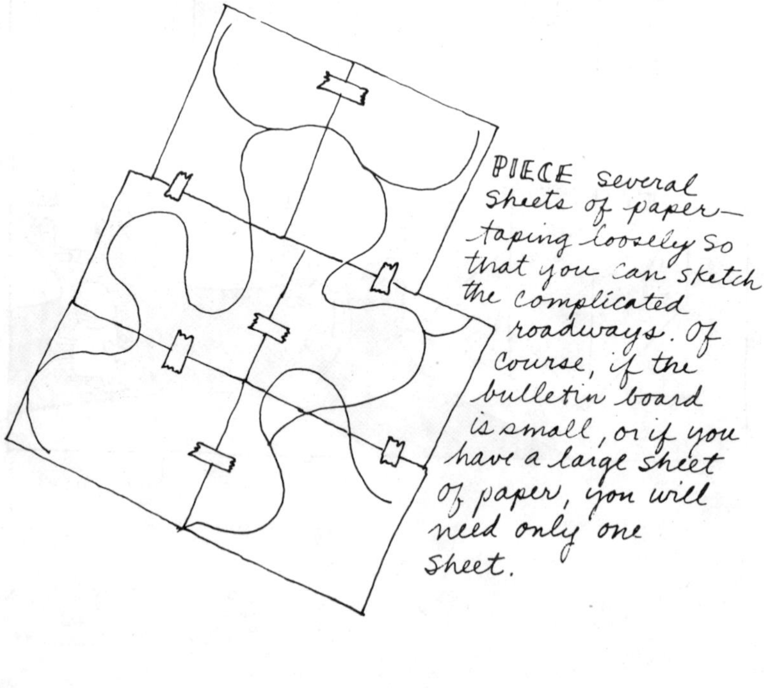

PIECE several
sheets of paper —
taping loosely so
that you can sketch
the complicated
roadways. Of
course, if the
bulletin board
is small, or if you
have a large sheet
of paper, you will
need only one
sheet.

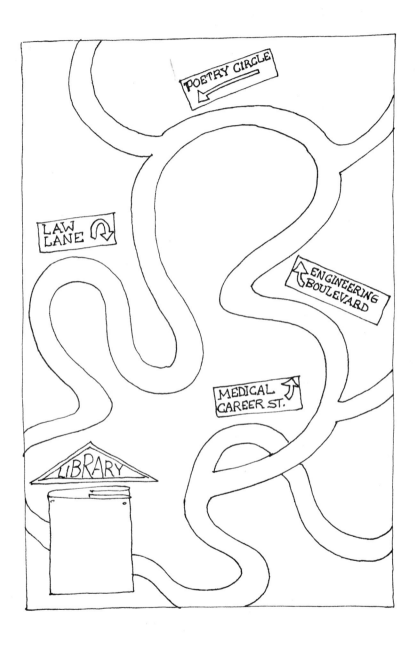

Books Are Open Anytime!

General reading; raising circulation.

Bulletin board.

Materials: background paper
tan and hair-color paper
felt pens
cut-out or pin-back letters
cut-out book

Technique: Cut out the whole tan head and neck. Do the entire nose and chin, don't try to truncate as shown here. Add hair and draw features. The cut-out book can either bear the message shown in the drawing, or the title of a good new book.

Adaptation: For a small display case, use a doll walking into a partly-opened book. Change the headline so that the pun word "nose" is now "knows." An alternative title might be "GET INTO A BOOK, AND YOU MAY NEVER WANT TO LEAVE!"

Classification System Cards

Familiarize users with your classification system.

Desk top cards.

Materials: poster board
               masking tape
               colored construction paper
               felt pens or crayons

Technique: Either draw and color the different pictures on a background color, or cut them out from different colors of paper. Draw on features and messages, then tape to easels. You may wish to include a translation of the numbers, or let your readers puzzle over them and look them up.

Adaptation: Interesting small case displays can be made by using real objects. Cooperate with the baseball coach for a uniform, bat and ball, and add a book on psychology and one on baseball for the first display. A sewing machine, rolling pin, baking dishes and books on aspects of home economics will make a good display. A twist on that idea would be to use antique or old-fashioned utensils and tools, and hang real lace curtains over the front of the case.

Bookmarks

Bookmark giveaways.

Easel-back display for desk.

Materials: cardboard, say 8½" x 11"
colored construction paper
felt tip pen
cut-out letters
gum wrapper, leaf, used cotton balls, burned
matchbook, uncooked spaghetti, cigarette butt
white glue

Technique: Attach easel back, as shown in drawing, to the
card. Apply letters on top section, then glue the
offending bookmarks to the lower part, leaving
room for lettering "NO," "YECH," etc.

To make the bookmarks, divide a piece of
paper into 6 sections with lightly indicated lines
which you will erase before having duplicated.
Draw, then ink, the various pictures and
messages on the bookmarks. Have offset in
school colors or various bright colors. Cut up,
only 3 or 4 sheets at a time, on a paper cutter and
display with the show card.

Leaf Book

Encourage reading of any kind.
Display case.

Materials: large sheets of gray-green, bright green, yellow,
        orange and brown paper
        2 sheets corrugated cardboard (carton sides)
        2 or 3 yards of black yarn
        pinking shears
        Phillips screwdriver or icepick

Technique: Cut book binding from cardboard, keeping ribs
        parallel with spine. Make book as large as your
        case will hold. Cut out leaves—making them all
        slightly longer and wider than the covers. Bend
        back covers as shown in drawing. Put all
        elements together and punch holes for yarn
        binding.

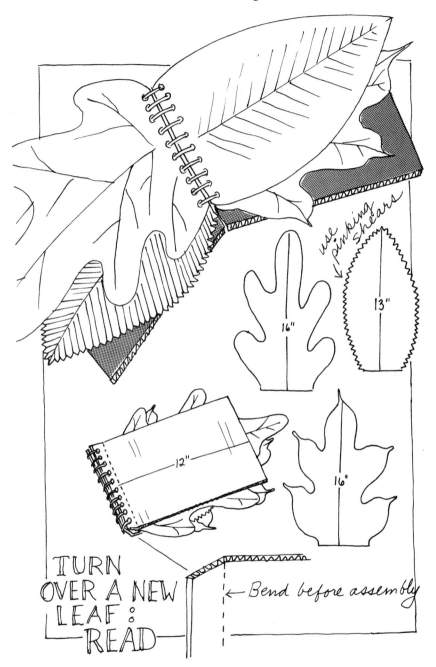

use pinking shears

13"

16"

12"

16"

TURN
OVER A NEW
LEAF :
READ

← Bend before assembly

Books, Memoirs, Biographies, etc.

General reading.

Bulletin board.

Materials: background paper
cut-out or pin-back letters
dust jackets

Technique: Put up the book jackets and use as many of the words as you wish, or certainly add more if you want.

Adaptation: You might simplify the message of this display and concentrate on only one type of book—for example, biographies and autobiographies. You can further define your display by doing only sports biographies or people from French history. Use pictures to supplement the dust jackets.

Or, base your whole display on the idea of bestiaries, and use a large picture of an imaginary beast.

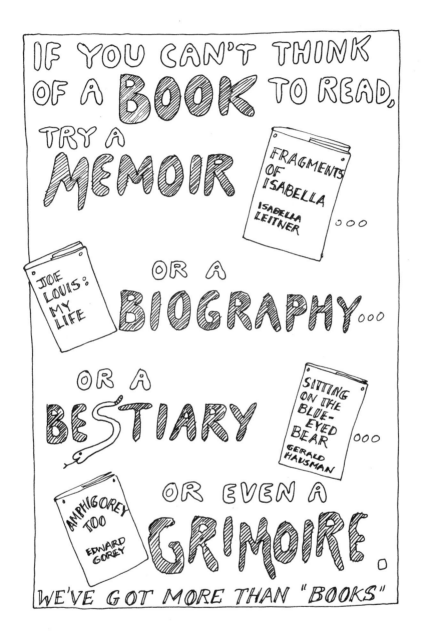

Famous First Facts

Joseph Nathan Kane's famous work; invention; reference books and almanacs.

Display case or pegboard.

Materials: background paper
cards
macaroni box
catcher's mask
eggbeater
ballpoint pen
toy car
beercan
matchbook

Technique: This is a particularly good display for pegboard easels because it is easy to attach the various objects. Use wire, thin cord, or monofilament line to attach the objects. Study the book to come up with items you can obtain easily, or select a theme suitable for a certain time of year.

Adaptation: Make this into a bulletin board display by using pictures cut from magazines, or select light or flat objects such as a piece of shell macaroni, a matchbook, a cover or page from a mail order catalog, a perforated postage stamp, an oleo-margerine box lid, etc., and tape up.

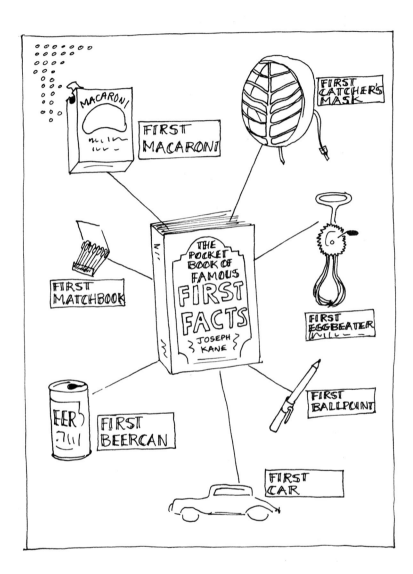

Which Would You Rather Read?

General reading; newspaper reading.

Display case; bulletin board.

Materials: background paper
2 rolls paper towels with printed design
paper towel holder
cut-out or pin-back letters
screws and screwdriver
books with same number of pages as towel sheets

Technique: Put up the background paper, and screw the towel holder to the wall. Arrange the rolls of towelling, put up letters, and print a card giving information on the number of printed sheets.

Adaptation: For a bulletin board, use a tabloid newspaper and two sheets of the paper towel with the headline over it.

Let a Book Lead You On

General reading; how-to books; humanistic studies.

Bulletin board.

Materials: background paper
big book jacket
tan paper
crayons or colored felt pens
small leash, or heavy yarn
straight pins
cut-out or pin-back letters

Technique: Cut figure and hands and feet of the book person from tan paper. Color on features and details. Attach to background paper, and fasten the leash with pins.

Adaptation: For a display on dog-training books, substitute a cut-out of a dog for the small human figure and use a dog-training book for the book person.

Cut out
two hands

ENLARGING TIP:
Draw long curved axis line.
Add 45° lines for arms; sketch
circle and long rectangles of torso
and limbs. Refine shapes and
add details of face and clothing.

Read Anything!

General reading.

Small display case.

Materials: background paper
2 #10 (very large) tin cans, empty or full
2 books, same height as cans
masking tape
cut-out or pin-back letters
real spoons, forks, dishes

Technique: Carefully remove the paper labels of the two
cans, and replace with same-size book jackets.
Put the can labels on the books as jackets. Put
up lettering on background, and either letter the
line "Big Selection..." on the floor paper, or cut
out and tape to the glass.

Adaptation: For a bulletin board, take a cardboard cereal box
and cut into a book shape. Draw lines for the
pages. Fashion a book jacket from a can label.
You can substitute any kind of printed packaging
for cereal and food—cut old record jackets into
book shapes, for example.

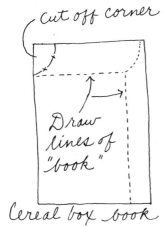

Cut off corner

Draw lines of "book"

Cereal box book

Catch the Big Ones

Library advertising; general reading; circulation drive.

Display case.

Materials: background paper
blue cellophane or acetate
papier-mâché boulder (see page 160)
brown, tan, green construction paper
monofilament line
crayons and/or felt pens
small rocks
transparent cellophane tape
kitty litter

Technique: Put up background paper (light blue is good) and attach headline. Put up the acetate lake on the inside of the glass, then add the brown boat and fisherman. See below for an acetate substitute.

TIP: Narrow strips of blue or aqua tape, laid in wave forms on the glass front of the case, are good substitutes for colored acetate.

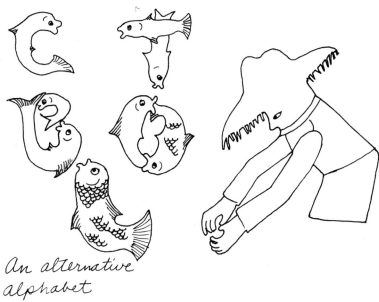

An alternative alphabet

Word Bird

General reading; dictionary usage; Thanksgiving; library mascot.

Materials: ½-gallon plastic bottle (milk, bleach, etc.)
9 pieces of felt 9″ x 12″ in two colors (such as the school colors or turkey colors)
1 piece each of yellow and red felt
coathanger
needlenose pliers
masking tape
stick-on moving plastic eyes
yellow adhesive cloth tape (½″ width best)
3 yards thick brown or dark red yarn
needle and thread
white glue

Technique: Form the legs and feet from the coathanger. When you form the body cradle, test to make sure the angles are right to support the body. Tape (and don't stint) when you find the balance. Then wrap the legs with yellow tape. Make the suit, sewing (or, in part, glueing) the pieces together, as shown. Attach the wings. Make the head, and be sure that the neck is long enough to fit down inside the neck of the "suit," so it can be sewed in place. For the "Early Bird" display, use the yarn to form the "A B C" worm. For the word origin display, print words in grease pencil on the white plastic egg-shaped containers used for pantyhose.

WORD BIRD

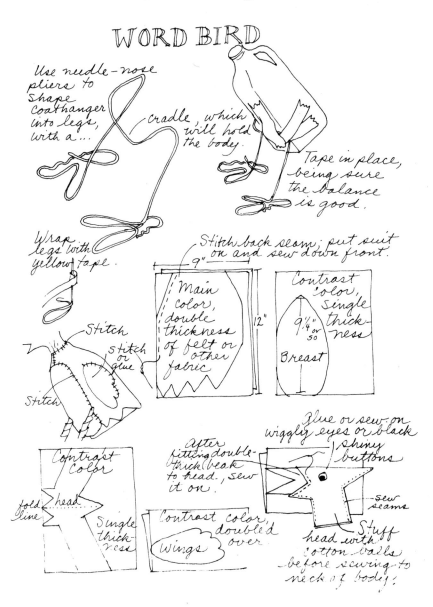

Use needle-nose pliers to shape coathanger into legs, with a...

cradle, which will hold the body.

Tape in place, being sure the balance is good.

Wrap legs with yellow tape.

Stitch back seam; put suit on and sew down front.

Stitch

stitch or glue

Stitch

9"

Main color, double thickness of felt or other fabric

12"

Contrast color, single thickness

9¼" or 50

Breast

Glue or sew on wiggly eyes or black shiny buttons

Contrast color

fold line

head

Single thickness

after fitting double-thick beak to head, sew it on.

Contrast color, doubled over

Wings

sew seams

Stuff head with cotton balls before sewing to neck of body!

A TURKEY WORD BIRD

back, double thick brown felt

breast, single thick beige felt

beige wings

head brown

comb and wattle

glue on felt feathers

very stiff paper or cardboard

overlap feathers front and back. Tape tail to body.

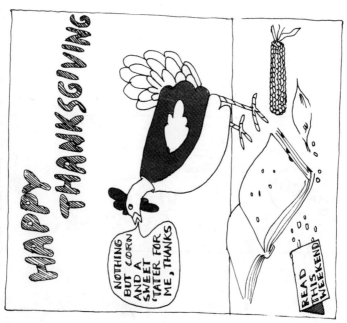

Dictionary Man

Encouraging use of the dictionary.
Bulletin board.

Materials: background paper
different colors of construction paper
cut-out letters or pin-back letters
heavy white cardboard or showcard paper
black felt tip pen

Technique: Cut Dictionary Man's book body from heavy paper or cardboard, including his hands, and his feet. If you wish to be able to use him in a display case, cut out the feet as shown with the dotted lines, and put on an easel back. Draw on hints of words and illustrations or use photocopies, and draw on mask and features.

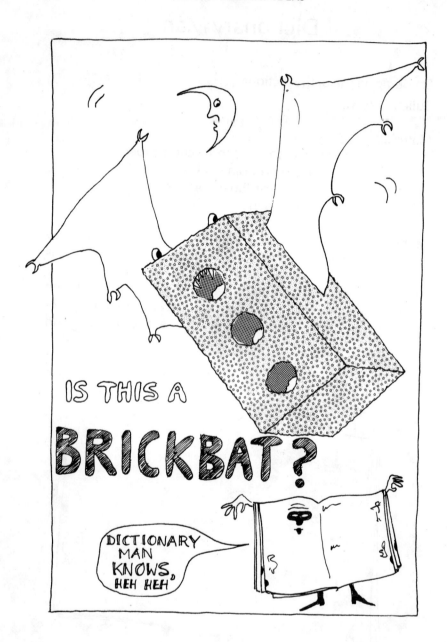

Word Play

Tout the pleasures of dictionary reading.

Bulletin boards.

Materials: background papers
various colors of construction paper
colored felt pens and crayons and chalk

Technique: Two examples of interesting words are developed
into displays here, but you can find scores of
others in the dictionary yourself. The secret is to
find eye-catching words. Everyone likes to add
zip to vocabulary. The "Patois on the Patio"
board has several easy elements: blue background paper on top; gray paper on bottom; cut-
out or pin-back letters; two white speech
balloons; a paper chain of flowers and extra
leaves; pen-drawn patio stones. The extra touch
comes with the *Corner Character* — in this case a
chicken. More of these follow. They are simply
cut from colored paper and detailed with crayons
or felt pens. The speech balloons are separate. Do
the "Graffiti" display on one color of paper —
perhaps a grayish blue. Use chalks to get the
effect of roughly-done graffiti lettering, and fix
with a spray fixitive borrowed from the art
department.

CORNER CHARACTERS

Rebus Reading

General reading and library use.

Bulletin boards.

Materials: background paper
colored construction papers
crayons and felt pens
cut-out or pin-back letters

Technique: For "Are you ready to read?" cut out the letters
and numbers from any color but red. The odd-
shaped piece of paper at top right *is* torn from
red paper. The ewe is black and white, and you
draw squiggly hairs on her. You may wish to give
a translation of your rebus, perhaps typed on
color paper, at the bottom of the board. Or put a
little note: ask the librarian for a translation. The
other rebus is a bit more complicated. Draw the
bin, the ear, and the letters and numbers. The inn
can be a magazine picture—perhaps of a colonial
house with your own printed inn sign—or you
can draw it. The knot can be drawn or made from
a short length of colorful cloth or heavy yarn and
pinned to the board.

Books Solve Puzzles

General reading encouragement.

Small case display.

Materials: background paper
jigsaw puzzle pieces
cut-out or pin-back letters and question marks
books/book jackets on coping, problem-solving,
or any other subject of timely interest

Technique: Attach lettering to background paper. Arrange puzzle parts on floor of case, having at least part of the puzzle assembled.

Adaptation: The use of jigsaw puzzle pieces can be very effective for bulletin boards. You can either assemble parts of a puzzle and glue to cardboard backing, or make your own as shown in the drawing. Another idea is to glue down a puzzle, with only a few pieces missing, and then to paint in acrylics or poster paint an open book over part of the puzzle. "Books can provide the missing pieces" is a good head.

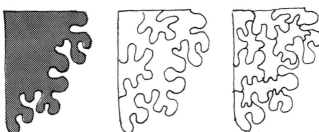

How to draw a fake jigsaw puzzle — start with corner. Make meandering lines, then fill in with more wiggly lines. This can be done on a magazine picture or art poster mounted on cardboard. If you plan to use it only as background, you do not need to mount, but pin directly to bulletin board.

Books as Defense Against Ignorance

Encourage the development of reading and writing skills.

Bulletin board.

Materials: background paper
various colors of construction paper, with red
     suggested for the book, yellow for pencil
cut-out or pin-back letters
felt pen

Technique: Cut out the simply-dressed figure, which can be male or female and attach to background. Cut out pencil and blacken the lead and add a pink eraser. Assemble figure, book and pencil, then draw horizon line and the feathered arrows. The headline can be cut from newspaper as a change from solid colors.

Adaptation: The knight on horseback from the display "Other Days, Other Knights" (page 144) can be equipped with this shield and lance as a variant.

Books Are Catalysts

General reading; chemistry books.

Bulletin board.

Materials: background paper
colored acetate (optional) in two colors
razor blade, single-edge
black felt pens
cut-out or pin-back letters
photocopy of two pages from a chemistry book

Technique: Draw the outlines of the vessels in ink. If you have colored acetates—perhaps you could borrow some old gels from the theatre, or use some colored cellophane wrapping paper—attach with dots of white glue over the vessels. Trim around the edges, using a razor blade. Remember that the acetate or cellophane is very very thin, so you don't have to press at all hard with the razor. If you prefer, color in the two large areas of liquid in the vessels and be sure to color the liquid being poured from one to the other. Because the subject of the display is catalysts, you must use two colors—one for the liquid in (and pouring out of) the upper vessel, one for the lower vessel. Finish by drawing bubbles, test tubes; attach letters and photocopy of book pages.

DRAWING TIP: It is often easier to cut out a whole shape, such as these chemistry vessels, and then trim off what is not needed after the pieces are mounted on the background.

A Great Lunch Menu

General reading.

Small display case.

Materials: background paper
paper bag
corrugated cardboard
green and yellow construction paper
plastic sandwich bag
plastic or wax apple, orange or banana
cut-out or pin-back letters
paperback book

Technique: Cut out bread slices from cardboard and lettuce and cheese or whatever from colored paper. Arrange in case and put headline up.

Adaptation: This is a good three-dimensional bulletin board because everything is very lightweight. If you can't find a plastic fruit, cut one out from colored paper. You might even do this display on a tray and put in the cafeteria.

Corrugated
cardboard
bread slices

Read for Others

General reading skills; story-telling; consumerism.

Bulletin board.

Materials: background paper
tan and various colors of construction paper
cut-out book
cut-out or pin-back letters

Technique: Cut out forms of the people, using tan for hands
and faces. The clothes are cut from patterned
paper or colored construction paper. Or cut out
faces and hands only and use a heavy felt marker
to draw the lines indicating clothing. Arrange on
the background with the letters and book jackets.
If you want, use cereal boxes (whole or backs
only) or other kinds of commercial packages for
the displays. A dogfood can label could be used,
for example, for the design with the dog. The
books could be on dog care, pet feeding, etc. If
there is a reading or recording for the blind
program in your community, or if you have
circulating records for the blind, the third design
will be useful.

Use a cut-out book like this in all sorts of displays.

To cut out a nice full-bodied heart, draw two circles, one half the diameter of the other, on a folded piece of paper. Then draw around them as shown.

There Must Be
Someone You Can Write

Encourage writing skills; books of collected letters.
Bulletin board.

Materials:

background paper
white, tan paper
typed memo and letter
job application form
mailed postcard

wrapping paper tube
pink sponge
yellow and black poster paint
½" brush

Technique: for the first design, use a large sheet of paper for the
stationery. Write "Dear" on it, and mark various punctuation
marks on it. Put up headline and bookjackets. For the second
display, use a cut-out paper pencil, or make one as shown in
the drawing below. Paint a cardboard tube yellow — leaving an
irregular area at one end tan. Insert a cone of tan paper, the
end of which has been dipped in black paint (or colored with a
felt marker). The pink sponge, cut in a slightly rounded shape,
fits in the other end of the tube as the eraser.

tan

black

yellow

*make
a cone of
doubled-over
rectangle of
tan paper.*

*Cut off some
excess of cone and
insert in cardboard
tube. Sponge
fits in end as
the eraser.*

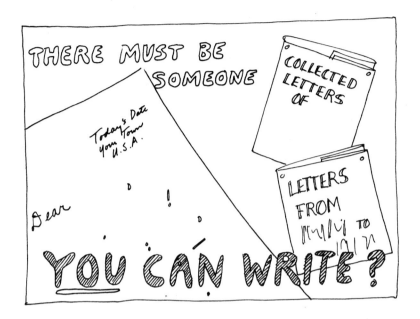

Play Pen

Encourage reading plays or tie-in with particular play.

Bulletin board.

Materials: background paper
tan paper for baby
brown, white, blue, green, red construction
    paper
diaper pin
4 different colored large plastic buttons
felt pen

Technique: Cut out baby and diapers and attach to background paper. Use brown paper cut in narrow strips for the playpen, or make with strips of masking tape. Draw line for button "balls" and pin them to board. Cut out baby blocks from various colors and letter with playwrights' names. Put up one or more book jackets.

Shakespeare at the Typewriter

Shakespeare plays; writers' techniques; typing manuals.

Bulletin board.

Materials: background paper
tan, maroon, black, white, gray construction
 paper
felt pen
cut-out or pin-back letters
book jackets

Technique: Shakespeare's hands and face are cut from tan
paper. His collar is white, cuffs and shoulder
pieces black, the rest of the tunic maroon. Draw
the features and the slightly-curled hair, and the
lines and folds of the clothing. Lay gray paper
over the lower quarter of the background, at an
angle for the table. Cut out the black typewriter,
or draw the outline with the paper. Attach Shakespeare next, then put up the headline and the
book jackets. If you wish to do this display
quickly, draw the whole thing on a neutral background, sketch in the color and add the letters.

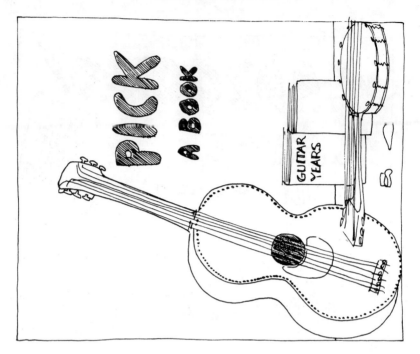

Choose Your Ax

Encourage reading of books on slang.
Display case.

Materials:　background paper
　　　　　　　real guitar (as shown or electric type)
　　　　　　　real ax
　　　　　　　cut-out or pin-back letters
　　　　　　　book jacket on slang

Technique: Cut out the two crossed axes and put up head-line. Arrange guitar and ax carefully so that there is no danger that vibration from footsteps will cause the guitar to fall over. A small piece of rubber mat, or a wad of florists' putty is sometimes a good idea to keep the guitar from sliding forward. You may want to include a card giving credit to the owner of the guitar (and the ax).

Adaptation: It is simple to make the display into a bulletin board, using cut-outs. You might want to add a photograph (cut out a magazine or newspaper picture, or borrow a glossy still short from a fan) or two of a guitar musician.

Pick a Book

Music books; guitar instruction; country and western.
Display case.

Materials:　background paper
　　　　　　　real guitar and banjo
　　　　　　　finger picks
　　　　　　　cut-out or pin-back letters

Technique: Arrange instruments, picks and books and put up letters. If your theme is country and western, add a western hat, or borrow some glossy photographs of the stars.

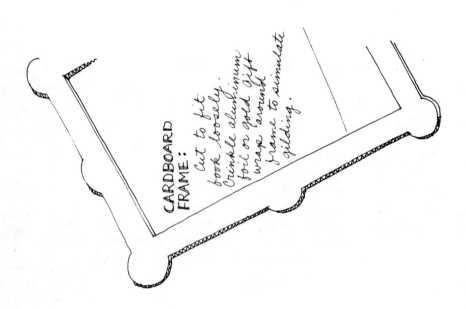

A Lot of Art Is Between Covers

General reading about art.

Small display case.

Materials: background paper
wood-grained shelf paper
doll capable of standing
dressmaker pins
large sheets of corrugated cardboard
masking tape
2 colorful book jackets
aluminum foil or gold-toned wrapping paper
cut-out letters

Technique: Construct two walls in the case from the cardboard. Cover with background paper. Cut out picture frames to fit dust jackets, and cover them with crinkled aluminum foil or gold-toned paper. Use the long-shanked dressmaker pins to pin the framed dust jackets to the walls. The cut-out letters are attached with transparent tape to the front of the case. Position the doll carefully, or use a doll stand, with the base concealed beneath the floor paper.

Read About Art

General reading on art; tie-in with art class.

Bulletin board.

Materials: background paper
large square of white paper
frame of wood-grained shelf paper
cut-out or pin-back letters
felt pens in various colors
book jackets

Technique: Draw simple pictures on white paper, and frame with wood-grained paper on which you draw loose scrolls and curlicues. Attach to background paper at an angle. Arrange headline and put up book jackets.

Adaptation: Make this a case display by using a framed painting, print, reproduction, hung on the back wall of the case. Cover the wall with tan or pale gray or cream paper. Add some paint tubes, a wooden palette and brushes in the foreground. Arrange books on individual artists, or how-to books on oil painting, watercolors, print-making, etc.

Read Before You Watch

Tie-ins with popular television programs.

Bulletin board.

Materials: background paper
local television schedule
black, gray and other colors of construction paper
photocopied pages from book
large newspaper or magazine photograph from the show being featured
red felt pen or crayon
cut-out or pin-back letters
book jacket

Technique: Attach background paper, and position a cut-out open book, with the photocopied pages glued to it. Cut out a simple television body from black. For the picture on the screen, use your gray paper on which you have sketched some figures representing the show, or cut the newspaper or magazine picture into a screen shape, with slightly rounded corners. Circle the show time on the schedule and put it up with the letters and the book jacket.

Comment: Time this display to coincide with the start of a new television season in late September or October.

Plug In

Tie in with books on which current TV shows are based; books on subject of popular TV shows.
Display case.

Materials: background paper
small television
12' or 15' extension cord
staple gun
2' or 3' of cord with plug
socket
aerial or coathanger

Technique: Form the letters of headline and staple the cord to the back of the case. Use screws or Velcro to fasten the socket to the wall. Tape other end of short cord and the real or makeshift aerial to the back of the book with masking tape. Obviously this display can also be used to make a case for reading *instead of* watching television.

Wireless

Radio history or repair.
Small display case.

Materials: background paper
45 rpm record
radio – battery or transistor
15 foot extension cord
staple gun
felt pen

Technique: Staple the extension cord to the background, forming the letters. You will be suprised at how the letters eat up the cord! A "W" only 5" or 6" high and just as wide will use up about 2 feet of cord.

Good Vibes

Solar energy; satellite communications; lunar tides; sun spots.

Bulletin board.

Materials: dark blue background paper
bright green and blue, yellow and white construction paper
aluminum foil
2″ or 3″ picture of TV cut from magazine
white grease pencil
cut-out or pin-back letters
black felt pen

Technique: Cut a general North American continent shape
from green paper and attach to the blue partial
globe. Glue the picture of the TV on your home-
town spot. Attach the yellow sun, silver satellite
and white moon and draw the features with the
felt pen. The various waves and rays are drawn
with grease pencil.

Harness the Sun

Solar energy.

Bulletin board.

Materials: blue background paper
yellow construction paper
brown felt marker
cut-out or pin-back letters
book jackets

Technique: The sun, with wavy rays, can either be cut from
one large piece of bright yellow paper, or from
several. If the latter, cut the circle, than add the
rays, rather like fringe. Attach to the background,
and draw the harness with the marker. Arrange
the letters and the book jackets.

Adaptation: For a display case, hang a large yellow cut-out
sun, cut from cardboard and painted, on mono-
filament line. Make a harness from thick brown
yarn, or use brown imitation leather.

Robot Reader

Science fiction, computer science.

Display case.

Materials: blue background and floor paper
2 cartons, one fairly tall, the other squarish
gray and black poster paint
wide brush and small brush
red paper or wide tape
2 burned-out lightbulbs, white or red
2 paper towel tubes or gift wrap tubes covered
      with aluminum foil
masking tape

Technique: Paint the cartons—3 sides for this display, but all
sides if you think you might like to use it as a free-
standing display later. Paint buttons and seams
with black paint. Cut holes in sides slightly
smaller than tubes and insert foil-wrapped tubes
as arms. Push ends of bulbs through small holes
in head, and tape in place from the inside. Put up
background with red zigzag and letters. Position
robot as if he were reading—a book on science
fiction or future shock or computer program-
ming, etc. For a great effect, get the shop teacher
to wire the robot so that real working lightbulbs
can be used!

Science Fiction

Science fiction; space travel; astronomy / Display case.

Materials:

dark blue background paper
tan floor paper
white, pink, pale yellow
  poster paint
½" brush
3 red and 6 or 7 green
  pipecleaners

foil star stickers
monofilament line
toy spacemen and rocket ship
several small rocks and
  kitty litter
2 Stryrofoam balls about 6"
  diameter

Technique: Lay blue background paper on floor—somewhere where paint spatters won't matter. Tuck newspapers around under edges, and tape flat with a few pieces of tape. Dip the brush in paint and, standing at edge of the paper, raise brush over head and whip your hand down. The brush will release spatters of paint—stars and galaxies. Keep it fairly simple, and don't try to uniformly cover the whole surface with splatters. Three or four trails—two in white; one in light pink, one in yellow, or mixtures of all the colors—will look best. To make the monster, twist the pipecleaners into legs and bodies and necks. Tape cut-out faces to the neck, and stick legs into the foam balls. Suspend the balls with line. Scatter kitty litter and rocks on floor of display, and arrange books and toys.

SPLATTER
TECHNIQUE

Loch Ness Monster

Pose the question about Loch Ness monster, or any other.

Wall case.

Materials: Pale blue background paper
blue cellophane or acetate
yellow, white, brown/green/khaki paper
white grease pencil
black felt tip pen
cellophane tape
double-face tape (or paste)
several small rocks
kitty litter
books on Loch Ness or other lake monsters

Technique: Put up background paper. Attach clouds, sun and fish to background. Put cellophane or acetate (or colored Mylar sheet) in front of case, just inside the glass. You may have to do one side first, then attach "Nessie," arrange rocks, kitty litter and books, then just before sliding case front closed, attach other side of cellophane.

Adaptation: This can easily be made into a bulletin board. The advantages are that you do not need as much cellophane, but without the light behind it, you will have to use white background paper.

Other Days, Other Knights

Show wide variety of books in which knights are featured.

Display case.

Materials: blue background paper
aluminum foil (quilted would be fun)
old poster board
red construction paper
black yarn
brown construction paper
felt tip pen
cut-out or pin-back letters
book jackets

Technique: Cut out shapes of knight's armor, then cover with aluminum foil. If the felt tip pen doesn't work to draw features and seams, use black grease pencil. Cut out horse's ears, eye area and lower jaw from brown paper, then cut horse coat from red. Make a yarn tail. If you don't use the red coat, cut whole horse from brown paper, and make a mane from yarn too.

Comments: This display can be used for a great variety of books, from *Connecticut Yankee* and *Ivanhoe* to books on the Crusades, or Tuchman's *A Distant Mirror*.

Homemade Furniture

How-to books on easy-to-make furniture.

Display case.

Materials: large sheet brown wrapping paper
large pieces corrugated cardboard
small doll with jointed arms
black felt pen
real hammer
small nails

Technique: Draw dotted lines on brown paper, as if they
were the plans for a chair. Cut out the two chair
parts; fold on dotted line. Push nails through back
to hold seat section on. Position doll as if
hammering, with tiny cut-out paper hammer.
Arrange hammer and nails. A few added swatches
of fabric adapt the display to do-it-yourself up-
holstering.

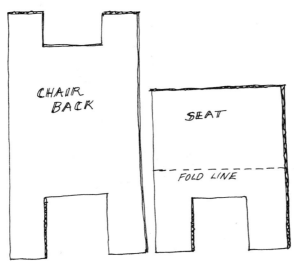

LOG CABIN

How to build your own log cabin.
Display case.

Materials: background paper
                    small or medium-size carton
                    about 40 fairly straight twigs/sticks
                    white glue/woodworker's glue
                    brown felt tip pen
                    green construction paper
                    double-face tape or pins
                    waxed paper
                    heavy weight
                    book jackets

Technique: Cut down cardboad carton, leaving only three partial sides and a part of the bottom to provide structural strength. You will be covering only two sides with twigs, and they have to be done separately. Prepare twigs so that they are reasonably straight and do not have lots of little side-branchings left. It is easiest if they are cut to the same length before you

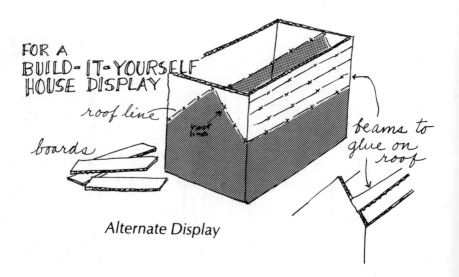

FOR A
BUILD- IT-YOURSELF
HOUSE DISPLAY
   roof line
boards
                                                    *beams to
                                                    glue on
                                                    roof*

Alternate Display

start to glue. Keep the door opening in mind. Cover part of the carton with an icing-thick layer of glue; wait a few minutes until the glue has begun to get tacky, then lay down sticks close together. Work as quickly as possible. When you have a section complete—say the lower half of the front, from the left edge to the door opening—put a piece of waxed paper on the table top, turn the carton carefully on its side, and lay your brick or other weight on until the glue sets. Complete in stages. Cut out fir trees and attach to background paper. Put up book jackets.

Forestry Can Be More Than Trees

Forestry; conservation; forest fires.

Bulletin board.

Materials: green background paper
gray, yellow, orange, tan, brown construction
paper
felt pen
cut-out or pin-back letters

Technique: Put up green paper. Sketch tree profiles on gray paper, the same width as the background, and carefully tear them out. This torn-out gray strip will cover approximately the top third of the bulletin board. Next cut out the flames, as shown in the folded-paper sketch, color the centers and attach over the gray paper. Cut out a simple teddy bear, rabbit and squirrel and attach. Put up the letter. You can also cut out a lower border of grass, using the folded paper technique. A simpler version of this display can be done by drawing the flames on gray paper with crayons or felt markers, then applying green paper over the bottom 2/3 of the board and using cut-out pictures of animals from magazines. Use bears, rabbits, deer, squirrels, but not jungle or exotic animals.

(A) is the green background. Layered over it are (B), a gray paper with roughly torn-out tree profiles and (C) orange flames.

Color center of orange flames red or yellow.

Don't Hike Without It

Hiking; backpacking; camping out; wilderness survival.

Display case.

Materials: large map
green floor paper
large knapsack or backpack
sweater, socks
water bottle
compass
cut-out or pin-back letters

Technique: Put map up as the background. This can be simply a road map or a terrain map. Stuff the backpack with newspaper and arrange the sock, sweater and plastic bottle.

Adaptation: By using a small knapsack, and eliminating the compass, this can be a bulletin board. The knapsack should be securely fastened to the board with long pins. Don't use where you can't keep an eye on the display, as it can be easily, if mischievously, torn apart.

Litter

Encourage proper disposal of litter and introduce books on subjects of recycling, etc.

Display case.

Materials: gray background paper
55" (or 36") jointed cardboard skeleton
monofilament line
wad of newspaper or mixed trash
real trash can or large wastebasket
plastic garbage can liner
crumpled drink cans, paper, bottle
cut-out or pin-back letters
black felt tip marker
books on recycling, litter, garbage, clean cities

Technique: Roughly draw graffiti-like word, such as "READ" or "BE CLEANER" on background paper. Attach to back of case. Using monofilament attached to skeleton's head and hands, suspend it in such a way that the legs are naturally bent. Suspend wad of paper or trash, and place trash can underneath. Put up lettering, arrange bits of trash, add books.

Adaptation: Instead of a wad of trash, suspend another cardboard skeleton or a skull, and use the words "Don't throw your health away." Display books on nutrition or sports or health. Another idea: remove skull from the standing skeleton, put it between the skeleton's hands, over the trash can, and use the words "Don't stop using your head." Display books on thinking, making decisions, planning a future, etc.

South Sea Bubble

Encouraging reading about an aspect of history.

Display case.

Materials: light blue or aqua background paper
green, brown, yellow, tan or pink paper (or substitute kraft paper for tan or pink)
white, pink or red balloon
black or brown felt pen, small nib
small drinking glass
drinking straw
rubber band
cut-out or pin-back letters
masking tape and double-face tape (or paste)
flowered paper (magazine ad, wallpaper, shelf paper, etc.) for bathing trunks
kitty litter
history book

Technique: Put up background paper. Cut out brown tree trunks and draw bands diagonally. Cut out and fringe 15 fronds. Tape to background. Quickly draw a few wave lines on background. Blow up balloon, tie end and further secure with rubber band. Draw closed eyes, nose line, smile and reflection "ear" with felt pen. Tape balloon to yellow (or tan) floor paper. Tuck neck of paper body under balloon, add bathing suit. Curl hands around glass and tape in place. Put water and straw in glass. Sprinkle kitty litter around like sand. Arrange book(s). Put up cut-out or pin-back letter. Add small 3 x 5 card with short explanation of the South Sea Bubble if desired.

Part IV

BROWSE FOR AN IDEA

Papier-Mâché Boulder

Display prop.

Materials: 4 or more ½-gallon and quart milk cartons
stack of newspapers
masking tape
flour (wallpaper) paste
large bowl
paint stirrer or old wooden spoon
brown, green, tan, yellow, black and gray poster
    paint
1″ and ½″ brushes
6″ copper wire or plastic package twist

Technique: Wash out the cartons and allow to dry. Step on them, crumple, bash, bend, then tape together in a boulder-like pile. Tear a good amount of newspaper into ¾″ to 1″ strips. Tear with the grain — usually top to bottom with large size newspapers, side to side for tabloids. The strips should be about 8″ to 10″ long. Mix flour and water paste to a fairly thin consistency. Many people add several squirts of white glue to the mix. Immerse several strips of paper in the paste at a time. The strips should be sticky and wet but not dripping. Run each strip through your straightened forefinger and middle finger. Lay strips on lumped cartons, following the craggy contours. In some high point, punch two holes about 1″ apart and make a wire hanger. Preserve the loop while laying the papier-mâché strips through and around it. Don't let all the strips go the same direction, but criss-cross them. Don't put too many layers on because the papier-mâché will not dry properly. Three layers should do it. Allow to dry thoroughly — at least several days. Carelessly paint the boulder light brown or gray.

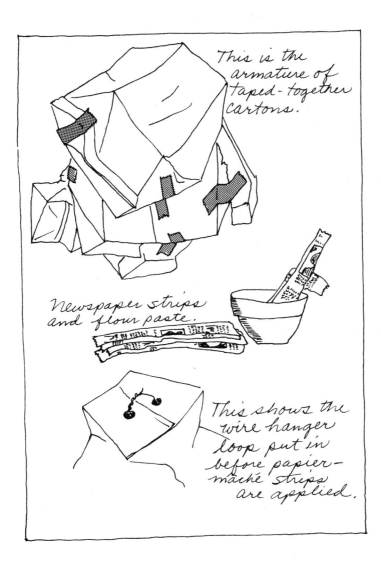

This is the armature of taped-together cartons.

Newspaper strips and flour paste.

This shows the wire hanger loop put in before papier-mâché strips are applied.

Dry, then use smaller brush, fairly dry, to stab and squiggle on other colors. Push black into deepest recesses.

Hanging Rock

Geology; geomorphology; gravity; science fiction; rock music; gemstones; space travel.

Display case.

Materials: dark blue background paper
gray floor paper
papier-mâché boulder (see pages 160-161)
monofilament line
kitty litter
small rocks
Velcro or staple gun (see page 12)

Technique: Suspend the boulder from ceiling of case. Use the Velcro Pinch, or staple the end of the monofilament. If you have incandescent bulbs in case, unscrew all but the one which is directly over the boulder. Or mask all but one part of a fluorescent tube with black paper. Sprinkle kitty litter and small rocks and arrange the book or books. For the second display, thread the monofilament line through the loop in the boulder, and staple it to the boulder at other end. Attach the line to the case-walls at a diagonal. Tape book jacket to line; attach others to back of case. Cut out a moonscape and draw the craters and some craggy peaks.

Sisyphus

Human rights; freedom struggle; job search.

Display case.

Materials: blue background paper
white construction paper
poster board
papier-mâché boulder (see pages 160-161)
monofilament line
white glue
masking tape
cut-out or pin-back letters
1″ x 8″ board in a length to fit diagonally

Technique: Put up background paper and attach clouds and letters of headline. Fit the board into the case. Put the boulder in place and tape another cloud over the monofilament line. Cut Sisyphus from cardboard and make folds. With a big dot of white glue attach Sisyphus' foot to the board. Glue at least one of his hands to the boulder. You will have to hold it in place until the glue dries because the chalky finish of the poster paint will resist a good attachment. You may, after taking this display apart, have to retouch a spot on the boulder with paint.

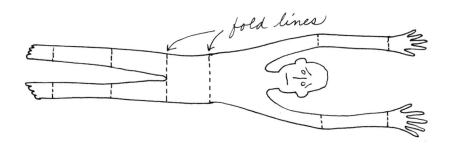

Body Language

Body language books; courtship of birds; identity crises.

Bulletin board.

Materials: blue background paper
yellow, red, tan, green construction paper
crayons
felt pen
book jackets
real feathers, if available

Technique: Sketch bird and female forms, as shown in the lower drawing, on colored paper. Refine the drawings, ink the outlines, and cut out. Give the yellow bird some extra green feathers, color some markings. Color a pattern on the woman's dress. Either use cut-out feather plumes for both, or put up real feathers. Add red hearts and question marks, and put up book jackets. If you use this display for books on finding identity, etc., one suggested—if obvious—headline is "Birds of a Feather..."

DRAWING TIP:
Simplify the more complex or detailed elements into circles and ovals. Use light pencil lines and then refine shapes.

Is Your Final Decision "Maybe"?

Decision-making.

Bulletin board.

Materials: background paper
1 sheet tan paper
felt pens or crayons
cut-out or pin-back letters
photocopy of pages from book showing how to
make intelligent decisions.

Technique: Cut the two joined figures each pulling in the
opposite direction, from a folded piece of tan
paper, as shown below in the drawing. Arrange
figures, with inked features and clothing, and put
up letters and book jacket.

Masks

Masks; costumes; identity; disguise; Halloween.

Bulletin board.

Materials: background paper
various colors of construction paper
yarn
book jacket

Technique: Cut out the mask shape and punch ear holes. From other colors cut fringey beard layers and wiggly hair, nose and eyebrows. The nose can be laid on flat, or you can make it three-dimensional by bowing it out as you glue down the edges. Knot one end of the two pieces of yarn and thread through ear holes.

Beard fringe

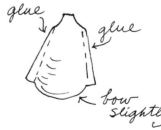

Part V

ALL AROUND HEALTH

Feeling Trapped?

Identity crisis; job-searching; entomology; territorial rights; higher education.

Small display case.

Materials: background paper
15 yards, at least, white yarn, cord or string
various colors of construction paper
crayons and felt pen
Velcro (dots or strips)
book jackets

Technique: Using the Velcro Pinch (see page 12), secure the ends of the basic spoke framework. Tie the center. With a simple slip knot, make the other rim of the web, leaving the yarn somewhat lax. Add the 12 or so additional partial spokes and complete the web. Center the black spider and add the other insects. For displays about books on human problems, use the small human figure. Other headlines are: ETYMOLOGY IS THE STUDY OF WORDS...ENTOMOLOGY IS THE STUDY OF "ENTS" AND OTHER BUGS; and INVASION OF TERRITORY.

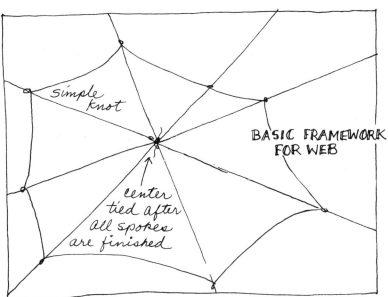

Note the irregular spacing of the spokes and the relative laxness of the yarn.

Out of Body Experiences

Introduce one aspect of parapsychology.

Bulletin board.

Materials: background papers—walls and floor
white, blue, flowered/printed paper
magazine picture of a chair
felt tip pen

Technique: Cut out paper for walls, angling one side. Tape or glue over floor paper, which can be magazine picture of carpeting, wooden flooring, or can be wood-grained shelf paper. Next put the bed clothes and pillow forms up. Cut out the two figures, making sure that it is easily understood that both are the same person. This can be done by matching pajamas and hair style. Add books jackets, then put on lettering—either done with the felt pen right over the blanket and in a balloon, or with cut-out or pin-back letters. Draw on lines for edge of walls, corner and the movement lines for the upper figure.

Profiles

Animal stories; pet care; dreams; primitive art; design.
Bulletin board.

Materials: black background paper
several bright colors construction paper
black felt pen
glue

Technique: Cut out figures (which may be overlapped, as shown below) and arrange. Draw on the simplest of details — nothing more than eyes and mouths.

Adaptation: This is also a very effective background for a display case. You may use colored construction paper cut-outs, or draw the outlines on the black paper with a white grease pencil. The latter technique gives a primitive, rock-painting look.

Dreams

Dream analysis; dream journals; Freud.
Bulletin board.

Materials: white background paper
tan, cream, blue paper
pencil
notebook
white glue or all-purpose cement
cut-out or pin-back letters

Technique: Cut out the figure and draw the features. Insert the edge under the paper representing the blanket and place the head on an off-white or cream-colored pillow. Under the left hand glue two pages from a notebook and a pencil. Put up the featured book and the notebook, and letter the credits near them.

Wanna Fight?

Nutrition; dangers of food additives.
Bulletin board.

Materials: background paper
red, brown, tan paper
black felt tip pen
cut-out or pin-back letters

Technique: All the elements on this display are cut from paper—brown boxing gloves, red star-like form, and several other clashing colors. This is a good display for an article from your clip file on junk food.

Adaptation: Use real boxing gloves in a window display. Hang two sets of them, in opposing position, from monofilament line. *Or*, use the gloves and a new subtitle for books on human rights, fighting city hall, organizing community groups, etc.

Nutrition

Encourage reading about good eating habits.

Bulletin board.

Materials: blue background paper
yellow, red, orange, tan, brown, green, purple
and white construction paper
black or brown felt pen, pointed nib
white grease pencil
double-face tape (or paste)
2 drinking straws
book jackets

Techniques: Put up the background paper. Cut one white egg,
milk carton, speech balloons, plate, glass; tan
hands and bread; yellow yolk (or color with
crayon); orange carrot and orange; green leaves
(fringe carrot leaves); purple berries; red apple
and dish mouths. Draw roundish eyes on everything with white grease pencil and felt pen. Add
pen marks for leaf veins, texture. Tape elements
to background, add balloons and letter words.

Adaptation: For display case, use real dishes, blown eggshell,
real milk carton, plastic fruit and vegetables hung
from monofilament line.

Drinking straw arms

Handicaps Can Be Overcome

Introduce books on successful people who have not been
  defeated by their handicaps.

Bulletin board.

Materials: background paper
paper in 3 shades of the same color—or
  approximations, such as gray, lavender and
  purple; gray, pale blue and electric blue; gray,
  pink, red
tan paper
felt pen
book jackets

Technique: Tear out two half-figures after sketching them
lightly on the gray and pale shades. They are
symbols for unformed, nebulous character. Cut
the victorious figure from the bright paper and
add tan face and hands. Attach to background,
and draw the features. The pale figure is the one
in the back. The headline can be lettered right on
the background, or you can use cut-out or pin-
back letters.

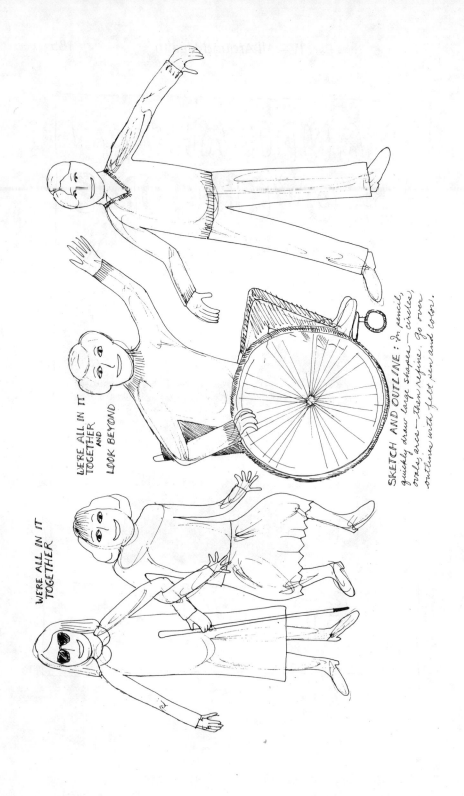

WE'RE ALL IN IT
TOGETHER

WE'RE ALL IN IT
TOGETHER AND
LOOK BEYOND

SKETCH AND OUTLINE: In pencil,
quickly draw large shapes—circles,
ovals, arcs—then refine. Go over
outlines with felt pen and color.

We're All in It Together

Encourage sharing life with handicapped people.

Bulletin board.

Materials: background paper
various colors of construction paper, and tan
     paper for skin
black felt pen
cut-out or pin-back letters
book jackets

Technique: On page 189 is another sketch of the different
people depicted in this display. Like everyone
depicted in this book, they are simplified, almost
cartoon-like in character. However, it is not
necessary to allow the cartoon to degenerate into
the grotesque. Just keep the figures simple
and the facial expressions natural. The wheel-
chair figure can be used as a male (page 186) or as
a female (opposite). For your purposes, any of the
four figures—three of which have disabilities—
can be eliminated to suit your needs. This is a
complicated display, but definitely worth taking
trouble over.

Whooooo?

Identity; bigotry; races of mankind.

Bulletin board.

Materials: background paper
red, pink, beige, tan, brown, yellow, black
    construction paper
14 9″ lengths of yarn
cut-out or pin-back letters

Technique: Cut the masks from different colors of paper. They
don't all have to be identical; in fact, it's better if
they're not. Cut out eyes and mouths, or draw on
with felt pen. Make ears for the book jackets.
Thread knotted yarn through each ear hole and
arrange the masks on the background. Put up the
headline. If you want to add some dimension,
put spots of glue only on the ears of the masks,
and when attaching to the background, bow
them out in the middle.

Vent Your Feelings

Books on emotions, assertiveness training, psychiatry.
Display case.

Materials: background paper
elbow duct of galvanized tin
cut-out or pin-back letters
black grease pencil
book jackets

Technique: Borrow a large tin duct from a local tinsmith, construction firm, sheet-metal worker, or builders'
supply firm. Draw features on it with the grease
pencil. Draw symbols for emotions on back-
gound paper, then attach the letters. Add books
or book jackets.

Skin Care and Health

Skin care; effects of diet on skin.
Small display case.

Materials: background paper
tan construction paper
washcloth
bar of soap
butter or margerine box
candy bar or empty wrapper
pile of potting soil or dirt
cut-out or pin-back letters

Technique: Cut out a pair of hands, and draw fingernails on
them. Attach to background, with the "or" and the
washcloth and cut-out water drops. Arrange the
books and skin-affecting objects in the case.

Addiction

All forms of addiction; the dangers of cults.

Bulletin board.

Materials: background paper
small jointed skeleton, or one to fit the board size
gray and green construction paper
soaked-off label from wine, scotch, bourbon
empty cigarette package
cut-out or pin-back letters

Technique: Arrange the skeleton, which may have to be partly disassembled, in a wretched pose. Make two paper chain leg irons from gray paper and attach. Cut out whiskey or wine bottle from green paper and attach real label. Arrange the headline and the words "BOOZE" and "CULTS" etc. Use one or more book jackets.

Coffin Nails

Anti-smoking.

Display case.

Materials: black background paper
corrugated cardboard
razor blade knife
skeleton figure, plastic skull, skull mask
large black cloth
several cigarettes and butts
dressmaker pins with long shanks
hammer
wide paper tape or masking tape
monofilament line
cut-out or pin-back letters
Velcro (see page 12)

Technique: Make six-sided coffin and lid from corrugated cardboard—either cut from a carton or from sheets. Assemble with paper or masking tape, and make hinges from tape too. Stick pins through the lid to hold the shortened cigarettes—the "nails." Hold lid up with monofilament line. Arrange skull and black cloth inside coffin, and put the hammer and cigarette butts on floor of case. The letters can be put on the back of the case, or attached to the glass.

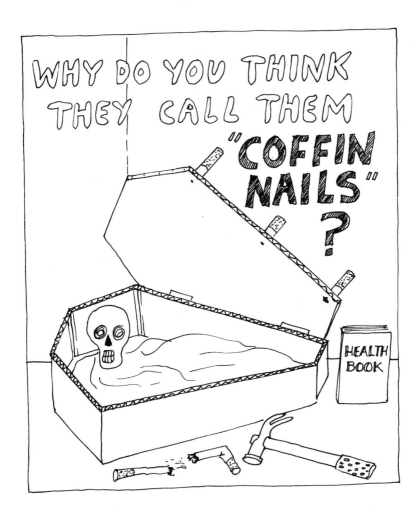

Anti-Smoking

Anti-smoking, health hazards; how to quit.

Small display case.

Materials:　background paper—black perhaps
3 or more lightbulbs, the opaque white are best
white masking tape
cut-out or pin-back letters
black grease pencil
3 or more cigarettes
all-purpose cement
monofilament line

Technique:　Put up background paper. Draw skull features on the lightbulbs and attach their cigarettes with all-purpose cement. Tape monofilament line to the top of each bulb, using a small piece of white tape. Hang from ceiling of case at different heights. Attach letters and book jackets.

Adaptation:　Suspend these grim reminders over a display of books on a file top. Or fit them into the necks of several weighted and black-draped plastic bottles—milk or bleach, for instance. Or, if you can remove the label from an opaque white bleach bottle, for example, draw a suggestion of a skeleton on the bottle, weight with marbles, sand, etc., and use as a constant reminder on desk or file tops.

Anti-Smoking

Anti-smoking books; health reports; how to quit.

Display case.

Materials: background paper
30" or 55" jointed skeleton
40" or so heavy carpet tube (or you can roll one
     from heavy paper)
monofilament line
cotton batting or dacron batting
white, black, and ochre/yellow-brown poster
     paints
wide brush
black felt pen

Technique: Paint ⅔ of carpet tube white. Paint the filter
end ochre or yellow-brown, and the ash end
black, with irregular edges. Suspend with monofilament line. Tease out the batting into long
plumes of smoke, and either attach to the background paper, or suspend with monofilament.
Arrange the skeleton with both hands on the
filter. If your case is long and not very high, the
skeleton can be seated on the floor of the case,
holding the monster cigarette between its knees.

Running and Health

Sports health; fitness; track sports.

Display case.

Materials: background paper
white paper
jointed paper skeleton (55" high is best)
monofilament line
heavy duty needle
gray paper, cardboard or even tar paper
pair of running shoes
cut-out or pin-back letters
book jackets
Velcro (see page 12)

Technique: Hang the skeleton in a running position. Put shoes on and hang shoe in raised position. Attach speech balloon to background, and add headline.

Adaptation: This is a simple bulletin board—just use a much smaller skeleton, and cut-out magazine pictures of running shoes. If they don't fit the direction of the figure's feet, cut out lots of them and make into a collage background.

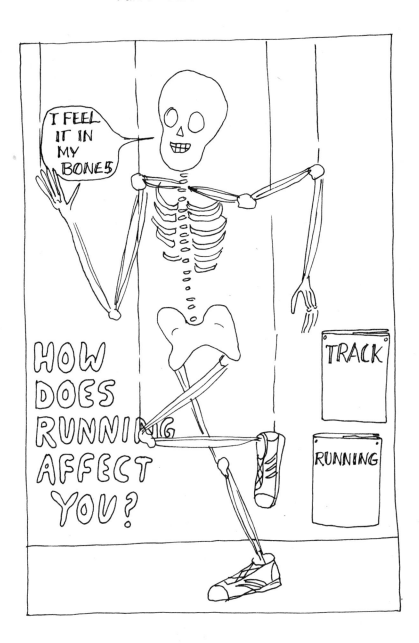

Part VI

OTHER KINDS OF DISPLAYS

Flag Pole Holder

Clamp-on block to hold dowel rod "flag poles."

Shelf edge.

Materials: 8" square of 1" board or plywood
¼" dowel rods, different lengths from about 24"
to 40"
C-clamp with 3" throat minimum

Technique: Have someone in the shop cut the square—or
several squares. Then ask them to use ¼" drill bits
and make several holes, going all the way through
at different angles. Make sure at least one is
straight through, and that one is an extreme
angle, so that a dowel rod stuck into that hole
would be about 30 degree off the horizon. These
rods can be used for felt banners or paper flags or
for suspending objects near books on the same
subject.

Adaptation: Another technique is simpler, but not as versa-
bile: tape a dowel rod to one of the handles of a
spring clip, which can be clamped to a shelf.

SPRING CLIP

ON
SAIL

C=CLAMP

SPECIALS ON SPECIAL EVENTS
BIOGRAPHY OF A LIFETIME
BIGGEST AND BEST

Felt Banners

Use with dowel rods to call attention to books.

Materials: various colors of felt in 9″ x 12″ rectangles
white glue
felt markers or grease pencils
white chalk or tailor's marker
needle and threads

Technique: Draw the outline on the felt with chalk or tailor's marker. Cut out, making sure there is at least a 2″ margin at one edge to fold over and stitch. Cut out appliqué forms and glue to the banner. Draw details with felt pens or grease pencils. If you wish to make a particular banner stiff, cut it double, from two layers of felt, and stitch together or glue with a slightly smaller piece of poster board between the layers. It is fun to design the banners so that there is a front and back view, as seen below.

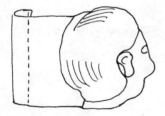 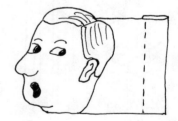

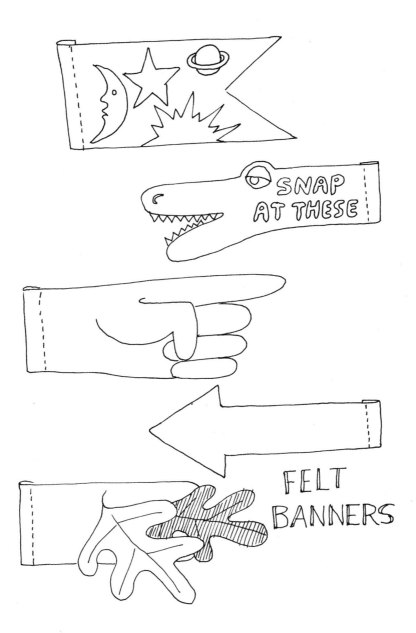

SNAP AT THESE

FELT BANNERS

Standing Animals

Display case figures.

Materials: stiff colored paper
crayons
lightweight yarn
glue

Technique: The three animals shown on pages 211 and 212 here are examples of how the forms can be simplified and adapted to allow them to stand. Cut them from stiff paper, draw fur and features, glue on tails and manes, fold along the dotted line and use in any display.

Adaptation: These animals can be made any size. The larger they are, however, the stiffer the paper must be. Of course, cardboard—either poster board or corrugated—can be used. One effective idea is to make all the animals from white paper, and use a white background. If you can alter the lighting in the case, dramatic shadows will provide the form.

Tips: When designing your own, the most important things to remember are that only one side gets a head, and that while the legs need not be in the identical position, they must be the same length for the animal to stand properly.

yarn
or
fringed
paper

beard
under
chin ↗

broomstraw
whiskers

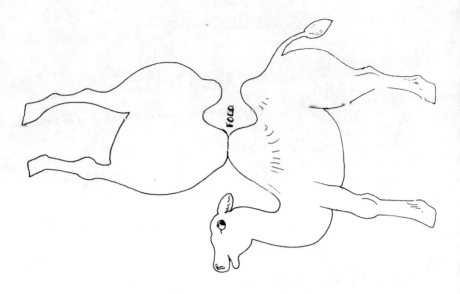

Jeans Book Rack

Permanent eye-catching rack for paperback books. (Can be used in display case.)

Materials: backsides of at least 6 old pairs of jeans.
long strip of heavy paper
heavy red yarn
felt tip pen

Technique: Cut jeans off a few inches below the crotch, making sure all are the same length. Remove fronts by cutting along sideseams. You can whip-stitch the jeans together, using a very big needle, or, if the home economics department of the school has a heavy duty sewing machine, ask for help. Yarn forms loops for hanging too. *Caution:* Do not use small children's jeans, or any others which don't pass the book-fit test before assembly. *Test all pockets.*

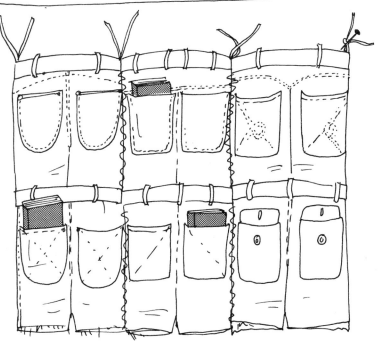

Off the Wall
(and onto the floor)

Signs for subject sections.

Materials: chalk
masking tape of tan or white, or
various colors of ½" or 1" cloth tape
scissors or razor blade

Technique: First, and most important, this is one display idea that you must test in a small area, rather like a hair-coloring product dabbed on the inside of your wrist for 24 hours. Start by asking the maintenance staff if they foresee any difficulties in laying down sticky tape which will be walked on and mashed into the floor for several months. Many floorcoverings can be easily cleaned when it comes time to take up your floor designs, and this includes some indoor-outdoor carpeting. Others, such as stained and varnished wood, parquet, cork, and some carpeting, are not suitable at all. If you get the go-ahead, chalk your design, then lay the tape down. The use of several colors can be particularly effective. *Caution:* do not use the razor blade to cut the tape unless you lift the very end of the tape off the floor before cutting.

Adaptation: Use this basic technique and tape designs on the glass display cases. Do not press down as firmly, and be prepared—if the display is exposed to heat or sunlight for any time—to have to remove traces with lacquer thinner (or fingernail polish remover) and a razor blade.

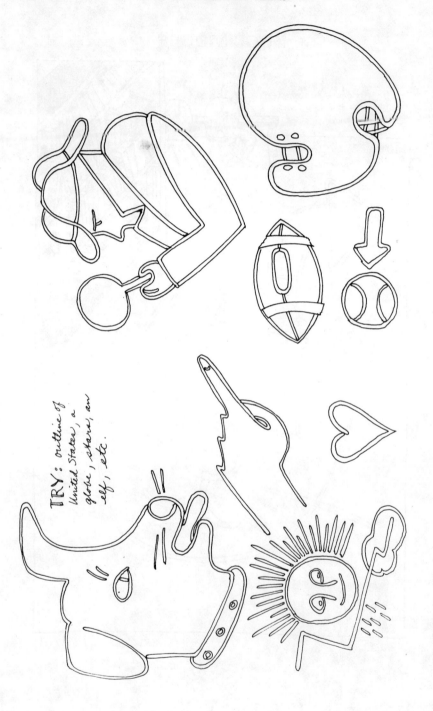

TRY: outline of
United States, a
globe, stars, an
elf, etc.

Book Mobile

Changing displays on various subjects.

Materials: heavy gauge wire
monofilament line
all purpose cement
pliers and wirecutters
12" x 12" board, 1" thick
strong headless nails and hammer
hole punch
poster board
crayons and/or colored felt pens

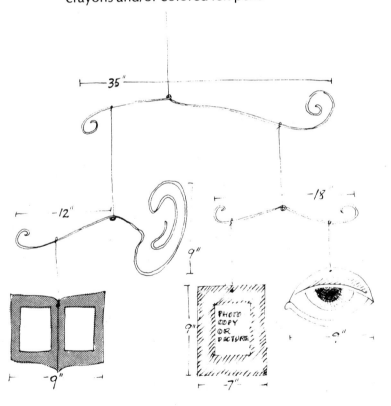

Technique: Sketch the ear and other curlicues on the board; then pound nails partway in, spaced every inch or so. This is your nail jig, used to bend the wire into shape. Cut eye, rectangle and book shape

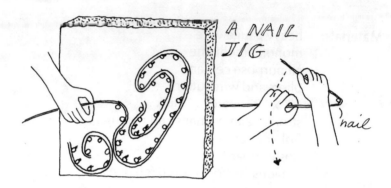

from cardboard. Hang the first long cross-piece temporarily from a coat rack or something fairly low where you can work out the balancing. Build the rest of the mobile, balancing as you go. After the balancing works, cement the knot to the wire, or use cellophane tape, to make sure the monofilament doesn't shift.

Note: the measurements in the drawing on page 217 are only approximate and do not include the extended lengths of curlicues. Exact balance depends on variables such as thickness of wire and weight of paper and cardboard.

Events Calendar

September

3, 1783	End of Revolutionary War
7, 1860	Grandma Moses born
11, 1862	O. Henry born
15, 1789	James Fenimore Cooper born
17, 1787	United States Constitution signed
20, 1878	Upton Sinclair born
23, 1800	William McGuffey born
26, 1898	George Gershwin born
27th	American Indian Day

Also during this month: Labor Day; Rosh Hashana (usually falls in September); first day of autumn.

October

9th	Leif Ericsson Day
11, 1884	Eleanor Roosevelt born
14, 1644	William Penn born
15th	Poetry Day
16, 1758	Noah Webster born
24th	United Nations Day
28, 1886	Statue of Liberty unveiled
31st	Halloween

Also this month: Columbus Day.

November

4, 1879	Will Rogers born
5th	Guy Fawkes Day
6, 1854	John Philip Sousa born
11, 1918	World War I ended

19, 1863	Gettysburg Address given
29, 1832	Louisa May Alcott born
30, 1835	Mark Twain born

Also during this month: Thanksgiving; Election Day.

December

1, 1886	Rex Stout born
8, 1894	James Thurber born
10, 1830	Emily Dickinson born
15th	Bill of Rights Day
17, 1903	Wright Brothers flew at Kitty Hawk
18, 1865	Constitutional Amendment XIII, abolishing slavery, ratified
21, 1620	Pilgrims landed
24, 1809	Kit Carson born
25, 1821	Clara Barton born
25th	Christmas Day

Also during this month: winter begins.

January

1, 1735	Paul Revere born (on New Year's Day)
5th	Twelfth Night
6, 1878	Carl Sandburg born
8, 1765	Eli Whitney born
12, 1737	John Hancock born
13, 1834	Horatio Alger born
14, 1896	John Dos Passos born
15, 1929	Martin Luther King born
17, 1706	Benjamin Franklin born
18, 1782	Daniel Webster born
19, 1807	Robert E. Lee born
19, 1809	Edgar A. Poe born
21, 1824	Stonewall Jackson born
24, 1848	Gold discovered at Sutter's Mill
25, 1915	Transcontinental telephone line opened
27, 1973	Vietnam Peace Pact signed
31, 1958	First American earth satellite launched

Also during this month: Presidential Inauguration Day.

February

1st	National Freedom Day

2nd	Groundhog Day
3rd	Horace Greeley born 1811; Gertrude Stein born 1874
4, 1902	Charles A. Lindbergh born
6, 1895	Babe Ruth born
8, 1910	Boy Scouts formed
11th	Daniel Boone born 1735; Thomas Alva Edison born 1847
12, 1809	Abraham Lincoln born
13, 1892	Grant Wood born
14th	St. Valentine's Day
15, 1820	Susan B. Anthony born
17, 1902	Marian Anderson born
22nd	George Washington born 1732; Edna St. Vincent Millay born 1892
24, 1836	Winslow Homer born
26, 1846	William "Buffalo Bill" Cody born
27, 1807	Henry Wadsworth Longfellow born
29th	Leap Day

Also during this month: Ash Wednesday (beginning of Lent); this sometimes comes in early March.

March

2, 1793	Sam Houston born
4, 1888	Knute Rockne born
6, 1806	Elizabeth Barrett Browning born
7, 1849	Luther Burbank born
9, 1862	Battle of the *Monitor* and the *Merrimack*
12, 1912	Girl Scouts founded
14, 1879	Albert Einstein born
15th	Andrew Jackson born 1767; Ides of March
17th	St. Patrick's Day
26, 1874	Robert Frost born

Also during this month: first day of spring; sometimes Ash Wednesday.

April

1st	April Fool's Day
3rd	Washington Irving born 1783; Pony Express began 1860
5, 1856	Booker T. Washington born
6, 1909	Robert E. Peary discovered the North Pole
13, 1743	Thomas Jefferson born

14, 1828	Noah Webster's *Dictionary* published
17, 1897	Thornton Wilder born
18th	Paul Revere's Midnight Ride 1775; San Francisco Earthquake 1906
22, 1970	The first Earth Day
26, 1785	John James Audubon born

Also during this month: Patriots Day; Daylight Saving Time.

May

1st	May Day; Law Day; first wagon train to California left Missouri 1841
4, 1796	Horace Mann born
10, 1869	Transcontinental railway completed
14, 1804	Lewis & Clark Expedition began
20, 1927	Lindbergh flew the Atlantic Ocean
24, 1883	Brooklyn Bridge opened
25, 1803	Ralph Waldo Emerson born
29, 1917	John F. Kennedy born
31, 1819	Walt Whitman born

Also during this month: Children's Day; Father's Day (third Sunday); traditional wedding month; school graduation month; first day of summer.

June

14th	Flag Day in many states; Harriet Beecher Stowe born 1811
15, 1752	Benjamin Franklin flew his kite
19, 1903	Lou Gehrig born
23, 1683	William Penn signed the treaty with the Indians
27, 1880	Helen Keller born

Also during this month: Children's Day; Father's Day; traditional wedding month; school graduation month.

July

4th	Independence Day; born on this day were Louis Armstrong 1900, Stephen Foster 1826, Calvin Coolidge in 1872, Nathaniel Hawthorne 1804, and Admiral Farragut 1801
5, 1810	Phineas T. Barnum born

12, 1817	Henry Thoreau born
19, 1848	Women's Rights Convention
20, 1969	Neil A. Armstrong walked on the moon
21, 1899	Ernest Hemingway born
24, 1898	Amelia Earhart born
27, 1953	Korean War ended
30, 1863	Henry Ford born

Also during this month: Dog Days.

August

7, 1904	Ralph Bunche born
13, 1860	Annie Oakley born
16, 1896	Gold found in Alaska
17, 1786	Davy Crockett born
18, 1774	Meriwether Lewis born
21, 1858	Lincoln-Douglas debates began
25, 1836	Bret Harte born
29, 1809	Oliver Wendell Holmes born

Manufacturers and Distributors

The following is a compilation of manufacturers and distributors whose catalogs I have consulted during the preparation of this book. The list does not, by any means, represent all the manufacturers and distributors of supplies useful for library displays, nor is it meant to imply that I have judged the companies which are included to be better than any others.

Some companies do not offer any retail or mail-order services at all. You must look for their products at stationery stores, teacher supply houses or library supply companies, but if you want something you cannot find, write the company for the name of a retail store near you.

If you order a catalog from one of the companies, expect to be asked to pay a minimal postage and handling charge. The $2 or $3 is money well spent, as the catalogs themselves are great sources of inspiration. When you know what new materials are being offered for sale, you will constantly be thinking of new ways to use the materials.

Before ordering, make sure you understand the minimum order requirements of the company. If you haven't planned a large enough order, try to cooperate with another department in your school or library for enough items to fill the requirements.

The final two listings are companies that do not handle mail orders.

Ain Plastics, Inc., 160 MacQuesten Parkway S., PO Box 151, Mt. Vernon NY 10500. *Mail order.* (This company had distribution centers in Manhattan, Southfield, Michigan, and Norfolk, Virginia.) The range of products includes transparent and translucent acrylic sheets; acrylic tubes, rods, geometric forms; acetate rolls and sheets—colored and clear; Styrofoam forms; metalized and Mylar polyester rolls and sheets; flexible vinyl hoses; self-stick vinyl letters; plastic-working tools; etc.

Arthur Brown & Bro., Inc., 2 W 46th St., New York NY 10036. *Mail order.* This company has a full line of artists' supplies, including every sort of paper; paint; felt markers and pens; brushes; letters; jointed wooden and plastic artists' mannequins; papier-mâché materials; templates for geometric shapes, symbols and letters; colored acetate rolls; metallic and Mylar rolls; opaque and overhead projectors; etc.

Demco Educational Corp., Box 7488, Madison WI 53707. *Mail order.* (District office in Fresno, California; dealers handling products all around the country.) This company makes and supplies all varieties of library furniture, equipment and display units; book dummies; acrylic and vinyl letters in many sizes; transfer lettering; pressure-sensitive, gummed and pin-back letters; construction paper; marking pens; colored adhesive cloth tape; opaque and overhead projectors; etc.

Eastern Artists Supply, 352 Park Ave S, New York NY 10010. *Mail order.* This supplier handles a full line of artists' equipment, including papers and cardboards; transfer letters and symbols; paints; felt markers and pens; folding easels; 12" and 15" jointed mannequins; papier-mâché materials; modeling compounds; bulletin boards; overhead projectors; mini-opaque projectors; drawing templates; adhesive cloth tape in various colors; etc.

The Highsmith Co., Inc., PO Box 25, Hwy 106 E, Fort Atkinson WI 53538. *Mail order.* This company has a full line of library furniture and equipment; display units; colored adhesive cloth tapes in many colors; textured vinyl tapes; transfer letters; die-cut holiday prints; self-adhesive vinyl letters; pin-back 3-D plastic letters; magnetic letter sets; felt pens and markers; wide rolls of colored kraft paper; construction paper; opaque and overhead projectors; wire print easels for table top; etc.

Little Kenny Publications, Inc., 1315 W Belmont, Chicago IL 60657. *Mail order.* Among the useful display products this company offers are "Write 'N' Wipe" spinners, score boards, playing cards; and self-adhesive holiday symbols and figures to be applied to windows and glass cases.

Trend Enterprises, Inc., PO Box 43073, St. Paul MN 55164. *Mail order.* Trend makes cut-out prints for bulletin boards in cartoon style; more realistic prints of prehistoric animals and the solar system; die-cut letters in various colors and printed patterns, including snow-covered "Frosty Icicle" letters; border design templates; etc.

Dennison Manufacturing Co., 300 Howard St, Framingham MA 01701. *No mail order.* This company makes a line of products especially for schools, but some of their other paper products are also good for displays. They have all kinds of paper including colored crepe paper in folded sheets, rolls and streamers; crepe paper printed to resemble brick and stone walls, and with overall designs of stars and stripes; poster paper; gummed kraft paper; colored cellophane rolls; pressure-sensitive seals—flowers, toys, animals, birds, holiday symbols; portraits of the Presidents and of famous black Americans; die-cut prints of food and musical instruments; wall maps; die-cut foil letters; vinyl letters; transfer letters; gummed foil stars; notarial gummed seals (resembling small circular saw blades); jointed Uncle Sam figure; etc.

Eureka Resale Products, Inc. Dunham Dr (PO Box 160), Dunmore PA 18512. *No mail order.* Eureka supplies retailers with a variety of paper products including pressure-sensitive and gummed paper dots, flags, foil stars, numerals and notarial seals; gummed die-cut fruits, birds, butterflies, flowers, patriotic symbols; insect and solar system prints; traffic symbols; self-stick holiday seals; jointed figures including Uncle Sam, Frankenstein, and various sizes of skeletons; honeycomb tissue paper 3-D decorations—snowmen, Santa, pumpkin, hearts, turkey, bell; etc.

Index

227